MW01120555

## ① JORDAN HOWARD
Regional Manager - Sales and Marketing at Oracle

It's on rare occasion when a person not only possesses the intelligence and motivation to be an effective trainer, but also that "like-ability" factor that makes them a joy to be around. Couple this with Earl's dynamic personality and his willingness to focus on helping people; it's no wonder the success of Quota International speaks for itself.

In all of the different sales trainings I have attended, there has yet to be one that has launched my career on such a positive and steep trajectory as Earl's. His highly effective approach to the sales cycle and well-rounded understanding of what needs to be done to get those "wins", separates his training from the rest, by truly being able to come through when deals need to close.

In my sales career (as a rep and manager) I've run into individuals for whatever reason, have that "it" factor. They're a "people" person; they get things done, don't waste time, and just "get it". All key ingredients to success. Earl is that person.

Simply put, if everyone had training from someone like Earl, no one would ever miss a target.

## ② MR. PÉTER VITÉZY, MR. MARCELL KARDOS
Budapest, Hungary

Earl is a karate master. He has taught hundreds of people how to combine passion with technique and how to become experts in a world where self-discipline and control are key factors to success.

Just like in sales. His thorough approach to develop the gamified Quota system to take salespeople to a level of conscious excellence all around the World. As a seasoned sales professional and leader he knows how to structure tasks and how to apply the flow approach to pipeline management. Quota is definitely the sales 1.0. Without it, expecting acceptable performance from a sales person is wishful thinking. The content is deep and detailed while the method is easy to adopt and fun.

The content in this book is a MUST for everyone in the world of Sales.

Peter Vitezy and Marcell Kardos
Budapest, Hungary
CEOs, co-funders of Actionlab Ltd.
Inventors of Attraction Sales and Decisionlab

www.actionlabconsulting.com

TEST**IM**

**MARTIN ALLISON**
Leeds, United Kingdom

A clear and understood sales process and structure demonstrates an organisation is both customer-focused and has decided how best to strategically operate. This practical and no nonsense book is authored by Earl Robertson and will provide businesses with a template which is proven and works!

Earl is a dedicated sales professional and I have had the privilege of working with him now for several years as one of his international licensees. I have seen him operate in several countries and cultures and with a great variety of institutions both academic and commercial and in all cases his preparation and professionalism is testament to his love of the subject of sales and respect for fellow humans.

Combine his knowledge of the subject matter with an understanding of pedagogy and gamification, his desire for all participants to benefit and his ability to ensure learning is relevant, meaningful, valuable and fun. This ensures lasting and effective developmental experiences. The many UK Quota clients and I are happy to endorse both Earl and the process as valued companions on any sales development journey you are embarking upon.

**CRAIG CHEVALIER**
Pickering, Canada

With the release of Quota®, Earl Robertson has delivered a book overflowing with the skills, competencies and common sense lessons that every sales person needs to know. I only wish that this book had been in print when I began my own sales careen decades ago.

Quota® Partnership Selling organizes and simplifies the sales process in a way that is truly unique and easily understood. It's the only sales program I've seen in many years that is an absolute must read for both the new rookie or the old pro.

This book is jam packed with the ideas and lessons that will take your sales career to the next level and I could not recommend it more highly!

ONIALS

## 5 · ASHRAF OSMAN
Riyadh, Saudi Arabia

## 6 · GEORGE ANASTASOPOULOS
Toronto, Canada

Back in 2011 I was looking for a partnership to expand my field of opportunity, and came across what I consider a brilliant way of building the new breed of sales management and professionals. We met face to face in Singapore where I received my certification as a Quota sales performance system delivery consultant. Earl left me with wondering a lot about my previous viewpoints on sales excellence.

Earl created a contagious culture that touches the people around him. He built, and is building an international organization that spreads the true and genuine way of carrying a vital job - Sales. The Quota sales perform-ance system is not only the best system in the marketplace, it is the most fun system as well. Quota started Using gamification technology years before the training industry started to embrace it. The result is generations of sales professionals and managers who have changed their adhoc, bean counting, shooting off the hip ap-proach to business effectiveness consultants who work along a solid methodology that helps them repeat their success and become elite performers.

This book is a must read for anyone working in sales, marketing, customer service. Anyone who faces a customer or one day will be, should read this book and thank Earl for that.

1954ashrafosman@gmail.com

If you want to become an elite sales performer, or build an outstanding sales organization with the compe-tencies to find, qualify, win, and grow business, then Quota and this book is for you. That's not enough for you? So you also want a proven sales process from Prospecting and Qualifying, through Needs Analysis, to Presenting and Approvals that makes the process of selling clearer and more manageable, while producing better sales results? Well then stop reading this and read this book. I've delivered the Quota Sales Performance Game and taught it at the university to corporate customers and students, from rookie to veteran in practically every industry, and everyone has always gotten piles of value and benefited in more ways than they originally imagined. So if you also want enjoyable, informative, valuable and maybe even a bit life-changing, skip the remaining references and go directly to chapter one.

## Valuable, enjoyable, information and maybe even a bit life-changing.

George Anastasopoulos
Founder & Head Coach at
Leadership Fundamentals Inc.

www.leadershipfundamentals.com
georgea@leadershipfundamentals.com

TESTIM

## 7  LILIAN BETH
Jakarta, Indonesia

## 8  STEVE TULMAN

In 2013, we at Sales Innovation were hunting for a sales system to represent in the South East Asian countries (Malaysia, Singapore and indonesia). We had previous exposure to many forms of sales programs in the past, both from our previous corporate experiences as well as our own training experiences. We always felt something was missing. We found the missing piece in Quota especially in helping sales managers become better sales managers. My belief is that if you can have good sales leaders, your sales teams will perform.

Earl embodies the sales process and leadership philosophy behind Quota. He is a man who partners with integrity, is encouraging, thinks quickly on his feet and acts quickly. He is quick to share his experience and always treating others with respect, yet courageously speaking the truth. All of this leading him to bring Quota to the all salespeople globally.

## Earl embodies the sales process and leadership philosophy behind Quota.

Steven Tulman is a passionate, goal-driven, and process-oriented sales leader and trainer whose ability to understand our business, and develop and execute the right sales strategy was critical in helping our organization achieve its goals. His leadership style and ability to motivate and inspire others is second to none. A pleasure to work with, I recommend Steven to any organization looking to drastically grow their revenues and take their business to the next level.

Gary Lipovetsky
President & Co-Founder
Dealfind Inc. & MenuPalace.com
Corporation

Success in sales is, in part, due to process and motivation; Steven has proven time and time again that he can clearly define both of these paths for success with the teams he works with. Steven has also been an advocate of including analytics in his approach to sales and leadership to ensure that progress and success are measured correctly.

Michael Kurtz
Marketing Retention Manager
Rogers OutRank

WHY ANOTHER SALES BOOK?
THE WORLD OF SELLING HAS CHANGED AND REQUIRES
A BOOK THAT ADDRESSES THESE CHANGES.

# introduction

Why another sales book? Surely there are enough 'how to' books in the market-place on how to sell? Why create another? What's different about this book?

## ...Good questions all....

Before embarking on writing this book, I asked myself these, and other, questions. The answer can actually be encapsulated in a succinct answer - the world of selling has changed and requires a book that addresses these changes. As the founder and CEO of a global sales training company, I have had the good fortune to participate in the education of thousands of sales professionals across many parts of the world today and seen firsthand how our profession has evolved.

*There are three distinct characteristics of selling in today's market:*
1) Selling, as a profession, is regarded differently in most markets (but the skill sets remain the same!).
2) Selling is less about the old style of relationship or consultative 'pushing' and more about partnership 'pulling' (more on this later).
3) Today's sales professional must be multi-functional in a variety of skill sets beyond basic product knowledge and sales skills.

When we examine top producers, across most industries, we often find very similar characteristics or traits. Top sales producers are: intelligent; resourceful; determined; well-read; inquisitive; and have healthy egos. They take pride in their skills and knowledge and being on top of their product knowledge. Most importantly, they understand that sales is a profession that requires constant training and development to stay at the top of their game.

## SO WHAT WILL THIS BOOK DO FOR YOU?

At its most basic level, it will acquaint you with the basics of selling. Regardless of industry or product line, your company has a sales cycle. While many companies have reduced their sales cycle to a finite number of steps, every sales cycle actually follows a consistent process. What is meant by this is that there are some specific steps your sales cycle must follow to ensure success.

For instance, you wouldn't submit a Quotation without first doing a needs analysis. You also wouldn't do a needs analysis without first interacting with your prospect and qualifying if they and the opportunity are worth investing your time in. The process we just described could be written as: Prospecting; Qualifying; Initial Meeting; Needs Analysis and Quotation - 5 specific stages of your sales process.

If you are already a seasoned sales professional, you may already be acquainted with your sales cycle, but the book will re-educate you to today's 'best practices; at each stage of the process.

As a sales manager, Essential Sales will provide you with additional tools to ensure your coaching and development of your sales team is in sync with today's best practices.

Finally, if you are a sales executive, you may want to juxtapose your current sales process and infrastructure against what Essential Sales describes. Only by reviewing your sales process will you identify the areas you can ramp up your sales technique and results.

In the 1970-90s, the Consultative sell became the norm. Salespeople were encouraged to shift their focus from simply relationship-building to "consulting" with the client. This meant salespeople were trained and encouraged to delve further into their clients' business issues, and determine how their products/ services addressed specific clients .Where time previously had been spent talking about personal issues, conversations shifted to a consultative dialogue that explored company strategies and directions.

The new millennium brought us to the present state of professional selling, the Partnership sell. Clients in the 1990s became weary of the continual probing by sales representatives ("Tell me about your business"), and began to look for representatives that already understood their business and could offer solutions based on industry insight. Representatives had to add value to their client encounters, or they were quickly shown the door. After all, which representative would you do business with? The sales representative who says, "Tell me about your business." or the one that says "Let me tell you about how other companies in your industry are dealing with the issues you are currently facing."

Partnership is characterized by: Understanding your client's business environment; being an expert on current industry trends and best practices; developing yourself into a 'thought leader' in your industry; and always taking a win/win approach to your business solutions. Clients that see ongoing growth and success based on your solutions will continue to be loyal partners for many years.

*By taking a partnership approach with your client's you will have ample opportunities to see how Partnership Selling will provide you with increased acquisition, expansion and retention of clients over the term of your professional sales career.*

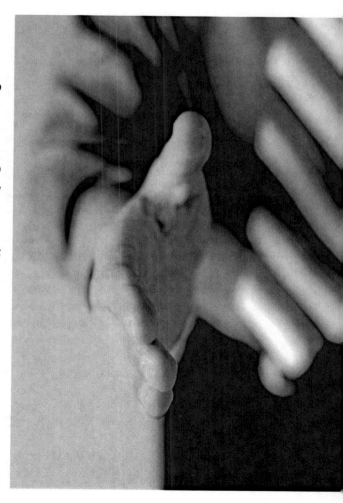

# KEY EVENTS OF THE SALES CYCLE

Please take 5 minutes to fill in each of the sales cycle events below and what type of action you might request of your own clients to ensure they are actively participating in advancing the sales cycle:

| KEY EVENT | CLIENT INTERACTION REQUESTED |
|---|---|
| Prospect | _____ |
| Qualify | _____ |
| Initial Meeting | _____ |
| Needs Analysis | _____ |
| Product/Service Demonstration | _____ |
| Quotation | _____ |
| Influencer Approves | _____ |
| KDM/Committee Approves | _____ |
| Purchasing Approves | _____ |
| Product/Service Delivered/Payment Received | _____ |

## STAGES (KEY EVENTS) OF A GENERIC SALES CYCLE

**Stage 1 -** Prospecting
**Stage 2 -** Qualifying
**Stage 3 -** Initial Meeting
**Stage 4 -** Needs Analysis
**Stage 5 -** Product/Service Demonstration
**Stage 6 -** Presenting a Quotation
**Stage 7 -** Influencer Approves
**Stage 8 -** Key Decision-Maker (KDM) or Committee Approves
**Stage 9 -** Purchasing Approves - P.O. Sent
**Stage 10 -** Product/Service Delivered Payment is Received

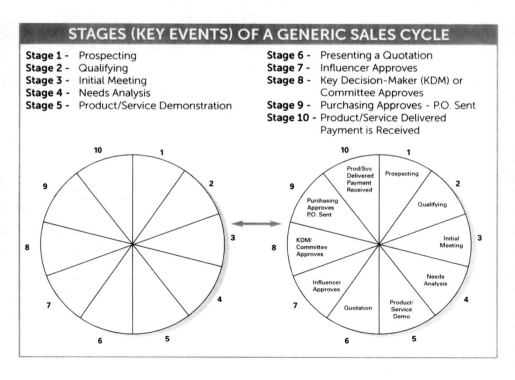

# Securing a next key event is likely the single most important aspect of any process-continued sales cycle. Ensuring your client is beside you step by step ensures the "close" is a simple step in a line of steps you have taken together.

Ultimately, we want our clients to be enthused about purchasing as we are about selling. The best way to accomplish this task is to ensure that your client is actively engaged in the selling/buying process.

To accomplish this result, it is critical that your client participates in each step of your sales cycle. For example: suppose you want to set up a meeting with other decision makers on a purchasing committee.

You could call these people on your own and request a meeting, or, you could engage your client's support by having him/her contact the other members of the committee and inform them that you would like to meet them shortly. In this way, your client is actively supporting your advancement of the sales process... and... simultaneously moving along the sales cycle.

| KEY EVENT OF THE SALES CYCLE | CLIENT PARTICIPATION IN THE NEXT KEY EVENT |
|---|---|
| 1 Prospecting | Your client is requested to visit your website to preview your company Clients are asked to confirm an initial meeting time/place. |
| 2 Qualifying | Your client provides answers to critical questions and agrees to send you an annual report or company information. |
| 3 Initial Meeting | Your client is asked to provide access to other influencers or decision-makers in the process or is requested to arrange a follow-up product/service demonstration |
| 4 Needs Analysis | Your client has given you permission to learn about their company and how your product/service could benefit it.  Needs analysis could happen on one visit...or dozens of visits depending on the complexity of your proposal. You should ask your client to arrange the meetings or notify co-workers in advance of your calling. |
| 5 Product Demonstration | Your client is requested to provide feedback, post-presentation. Clients could be asked for access to finance or purchasing contacts to secure budget or purchasing constraint conditions. |
| 6 Quotation Submission | Your client is requested to explain the quotation and purchasing decision-process. You should ask your client at this stage to describe "winning" criteria and when/where evaluation of the quotation will take place. You may request your client to arrange a presentation of your quotation to a key decision-maker (KDM) or committee. |

**7 Influencer Approves**

Within your client's organization there will be two key categories of purchasers. Those that influence the decision (positively or negatively) and those that make the final decision. It is not uncommon for the influencer to be the driving force behind the purchase, but not the final decider of whether the purchase is made or not. Ask your client who is who in their organization.

**8 Key Decision-Maker (KDM) / Committee Approves**

Final decision-makers within your client's organization will frequently be uninvolved with the details of the purchase. However, you still require their final approval to make the deal happen. Typically, KDMs are senior line managers (depending on product/service purchased) and have Profit & Loss (P&L) responsibility in their companies. They balance their purchasing decisions among a variety of other purchasing requests and look for the best return on investment.

**9 Purchasing Approves**

Great news! You have reached the stage where Purchasing is ready to issue a Purchase Order (P.O.). Once all parties on the "line" side of the business have approved, the "staff" or purchasing function gets involved. Depending on the type of business or structure, purchasing may "rubber-stamp" orders...or... have the authority to stop a purchase. It is always a good idea to find out which type of authority your client's purchasing department has and then ensure it is part of your sales process.

**Product/ Service Delivered**

You are ALMOST home...but you wouldn't be the first seller who did not get the order because of an unexpected budget freeze, acquisition or bankruptcy ... so sit tight until the payment is received. Ask your client for permission to follow up to ensure all internal details (P.O. Issued, Shipping Notified, etc.) have been managed.

# LESSONS FROM THE ROAD

Imagine two different travellers. They are both given a destination to reach and left to their own devices to find their way there.

The first traveller immediately jumps on a bus and begins the process of asking everyone they meet how to get to this destination in a new country. The second traveller sits down and plans the steps and modes of transportation they will book to get them where they want to go.

Two days later the second traveller arrives at their destination after taking a series of: taxis; airlines and shuttles. The first traveller is still on the bus asking for directions.

This is, unfortunately, what often happens in sales. Many reps meet prospects without a clear plan on how they, and their prospect, can work together and build a mutually profitable alliance.

However, the rep that understands the sales cycle has a clear objective each time they meet their prospect. They understand that the client needs to be involved at each step of the process and that they need to continually demonstrate how their partnership will result in the client achieving their operational objectives.

I recall two reps on a team I had inherited. The first rep had average results but was well liked by management and their co-workers. The second rep had out-standing results but was widely regarded as 'flakey'.

When I first worked with the two reps (separately) in the field, I asked them the same sales call preparation questions:

1) Where are we in the sales cycle?
2) What is our call objective?
3) How will we know if we achieved the objective?
4) What are the Personal and Organization Motivators of the prospect we are meeting?

**REP #1 ANSWERED**

1) Just getting to know the client
2) See if they like me
3) If they want to see me again
4) Don't know yet as we haven't met

**REP #2 ANSWERED**

1) Initial Meeting stage - we're at a 30% probability of closing this client
2) Have the client agree to a joint meeting with their Key Decision Maker (KDM) and advance to the Needs Analysis stage and 40% probability of closing
3) Prospect contacts the KDM while we are there to set up the meeting
4) Based on my research, this prospect is a highly detailed individual that doesn't like to take chances and follows policy closely.

# Time for a POP QUIZ.

The POP QUIZ will test your knowledge of the preceding reading and give you insight into how strong your sales knowledge is. At the end of the book, we will add up your POP QUIZ scores and see where you are strong and where you may want to re-read a chapter! **Good Luck! One point for correct answer.**

The 5th Stage Key Event in our sales cycle is:
a) Product/Service Demo
b) Presenting a Quotation
c) Influencer Approves
d) Making a Presentation

ANSWER: _____

The 9th Stage Key Event in our sales cycle is:
a) KDM/Committee approves
b) Influencer Approves
c) Payment Received
d) Purchasing Approves - P.O. Sent

ANSWER: _____

The definition of the Influencer in Partnership Selling is the:
a) External referral giver
b) Final Decision Maker
c) Internal (client company) influencer
d) None of the above

ANSWER: _____

Examples of prospect sources include:
a) Trade shows
b) Trade publications
c) Social contacts
d) All of the above

ANSWER: _____

True or False: Relationship Selling is the contemporary way to sell to clients?
T) True
F ) False

ANSWER: _____

STAGE 1

Prospecting

THE 'ART' AND 'SCIENCE' OF SELLING
ARE CRITICAL TO SALES SUCCESS

# stage one

## PROSPECTING

As professional salespeople, you are the elite of your industry. It is your responsibility to acquire new clients, expand business within existing accounts and ensure retention of customers. In other words, how effectively you prospect, qualify, analyze, negotiate, present and close business will have a direct impact on your company's growth and success.

Throughout this book, you will encounter opportunities to affect each of these key responsibilities by your own decision and efforts. As in real life, the decisions you make will have a direct and quantifiable impact on your own sales performance success.

Before we begin reviewing the key competencies required in today's market-place, we have a question for you..... Is selling an art or a science?

Successful salespeople often debate what they attribute their success to. In some cases, it is the appropriate use of skills at the opportune time. For others it is the relationship they have cultivated between themselves and their clients. And for others still, it is a combination of their sales skills (science) and the rapport (art) they have with their customer.

The answer, of course, is that success can occur anywhere on the spectrum between the two points of view. Both the 'art' and 'science' of selling are critical to sales success. Therefore the answer is - Both!

This book will explore both aspects of successful selling and how you can enhance your own abilities in both arenas.

Even the most ardent of sales professionals will admit that training and coaching have had a significant impact on their sales success. This book will provide you with essential tools to monitor your own performance, and introduce new concepts to guide you toward consistent quota achievement.

One area we need to review before exploring the various competencies professional sales professionals need to excel at is a major trend that is impacting sales across the globe...that is the client's expectation that their representative be a 'partner' and provide them with key insights that can help them grow and prosper.

# We call this:

### Partnership Selling – The Evolution of Selling

When we look at the evolution of sales training programs over the last 50 years, we see that selling has evolved significantly. Originally, sales were considered a Relationship activity. Selling in the 1950-70s was largely an activity that focused on building a relationship with the customer and being the provider of choice. It was not unusual for salespeople to spend hours of extra-curricular time socializing with their clients and enjoying a variety of non-business activities together.

the client's expectation is that their representative is a partner and can provide them with key insights that will help them grow and prosper.

# PROSPECTING

*Often described as the most difficult stage of selling. Prospecting, by its very nature, involves more refection than acceptance. Your prospect will be more open to taking your call or meeting with you when referred to them by a common contact. Similarly as with inbound leads, the follow-up should be prompt. The longer you wait, the more likely they are to either lose interest in hearing about your solution, or they may have already found another company to work with.*

Some key tips to prospecting are:

## 1) DEFINE YOUR TARGET MARKET:

Often times businesses and sales professionals spend their time going after the wrong target markets. These organizations go after markets that are unlikely to buy from them for four main reasons; they are either too small to afford the services, they are too big/small and require a more/less advanced solution. The problem that the solution addresses is not big enough for them to justify spending money on resolving, or they simply don't have the budget at this time. To avoid these pitfalls you'll first need to determine what industries or groups have the biggest and most urgent/painful challenges that your solution can help them resolve. This will define your primary target industries. Those are the industries that you should focus on since they're your lowest hanging fruit.

Next you'll need to understand the size of the organizations within your primary target industries that are most likely to buy from you based on price, complexity of your solution, and reputation of your company. This will define your target companies.

Finally, when prospecting, and even when dealing with inbound leads, you need to determine what are the right buying centres for your kind of solution, and what roles within those buying centres are directly involved in making the purchasing decisions. These will be your primary target buying centres.

These primary target prospects are going to be the easiest customers to acquire. Don't confuse that with being EASY customers to acquire... those are much rarer gems to find.

Now that you've got your target market, comprised of primary target organizations and buying centres, you're ready to start prospecting into them.

## 2) START WITH THE TOP DECISION MAKER:

ALWAYS start at the top! Once you determined what industries, companies, and buying centres you need to target, you then need to be prepared to reach out to the top person in those buying centres. It can be scary calling into a CEO, or a top level VP or Director at an organization. But it's the fastest way to making a sale.

If you can't get through to them then you can work your way down and find out who you can speak with that works directly with the CEO, VP or Director, and who's opinions they trust. This person will be your "Champion" or "Key Influencer" going forward in your sales process.

In the case of an inbound lead, speak with the person who reached out to you, but keep in mind that just because they reached out to you doesn't mean they are the decision maker or influencer. Be respectful and address their questions, but find out if they are in fact the real decision maker or a key influencer and if they're not, then find out who is and try to get a meeting with them.

## 3) CHOOSING THE BEST METHODS TO PROSPECT:

There are many different tools and methods that we as sales professionals and entrepreneurs can use when prospecting for new business. Depending on the nature of your product/service and your target demographic, you will find that some methods work better than others.

*Some methods that have been found to be most effective in various instances:*
- **Advertising & Lead Generation:** Ensure that your marketing and lead generation efforts are targeting the right demographic in the right ways. You need to ensure that your website and landing pages have effective call-to-action functions and are properly optimized for search engines. This helps your chances of appearing in Google search results under the specific terms that will generate the most inbound leads for you. A well-managed Pay Per Click campaign is a quicker and more direct way of generating qualified inbound leads when you want them. Ensuring that you have a solid reputation online with a significant amount of customer reviews will directly increase the number of inbound leads that you generate as more and more people are turning to review sites like Yelp, Google+, and N49 when searching for possible vendors. Encourage your customers to review your services online whenever possible.

- **Handling Inbound Leads:** With inbound and warm leads, time is of the essence. The longer you wait to call them back the less likely you are to reach them or make a sale. In fact if you respond to an inbound lead 2 hours after the lead was sent, you are 15% less likely to close that deal. This is because people will usually send requests to multiple vendors and quite often the first vendor that responds gets the deal. This is especially true when you are dealing with a smaller company, although even with larger companies, the sooner you respond to a lead, the more likely you are to close it.
- **LinkedIn (and a few other social media sites):** This is a great way to find and connect with decision makers in the companies that you're targeting. You can search by company name, by industry, by geography, by title, and various other search criteria. You can then either invite them to join your network, send them a message requesting a chat, or see if you have any mutual connections that you can request an introduction from. Many people in upper management know others in similar roles at other organizations. You'll find that it becomes easier to get warm introductions to your prospects as you start

## 4) FOLLOW A PROSPECTING SCHEDULE:

Having a daily or weekly schedule detailing what prospecting activities you will perform at which times and on which days, will help you stay on track and help keep the top of your funnel full. Because prospecting can be difficult and has its ups and downs, it helps to have set times when you know you have to do it and sticking to those times as much as possible. I suggest prospecting in the first quarter and last quarter of your day and also during lunchtime. The rest of your day should be split between admin, account management, following up on previous conversations, meeting preparation, prospecting preparation, data-mining, and so on.

## 5) ALWAYS SECURE A NEXT STEP DATE AND SPECIFY WHAT THOSE NEXT STEPS WILL BE

This is both the easiest and one of the most forgotten components of an effective prospecting process. It not only applies to prospecting, but it applies to every stage of the sales cycle, at every interaction that you have with your prospects. Here's how to apply it when prospecting.

- When finally getting through to the decision maker or key influencer, ALWAYS be sure to specify a specific next step date, the specific goals that you wish to achieve before or on that date, and what actions both you and your prospect are responsible for prior to that date.

If your next step is to book a meeting, then book that meeting and inform your prospect of what will be discussed at the meeting and what you hope to achieve by the end of that meeting. Also outline anything that you or your prospect needs to do in preparation for the meeting. If your next step is to send them an email and call them back, then don't tell them that you will call back sometime later in the week. Agree on a specific day and time with your prospect and follow through with your follow-up call on that day and time.

## When securing the next step, be specific. It will help you and your prospect stay on track.

If you don't start at the top, and instead start with a lower-level employee, you will most likely have many great and lengthy conversations, but at the end of the day the person you've spent your time speaking with has little to no say in the decisions being made at the organization. You will most likely take this person through the entire sales cycle, spending days, weeks, or even months of your valuable time pitching to them. Then when it comes down to getting a decision from them you will probably spend days or weeks chasing them on the phone, sending them countless emails and either never getting a reply and giving up, or being told that they are not interested in your solution. It's not because they're not interested, it's because they have no input. You'll have to start all over again at this point, so why not do it right from the beginning?

There are few things more demoralizing to a sales professional or small business owner than wasting months going through a sales cycle and having it fall apart at the end because they haven't been speaking to the right person. It has been said the most stressful aspect to business development is the initial approach, or the prospecting effort for new business. The rejection rate is high, and no one enjoys having his or her efforts turned down or rebuffed.

# USE OF SOCIAL MEDIA TO SOURCE LEADS

Social Media is a contemporary and essential tool for any sales professional tasked with business development responsibilities. Although there are a myriad of sites available to connect with both prospects and clients, there are a few front-runners in this field: Facebook; LinkedIn and Twitter. Whichever (or all!) of the social media sites you register on, here are a few tips on how to maximize your lead generation:

- Identify key clients that would be willing to give you a reference on your site
- Reach out to every new prospect by sending them your link and asking for theirs in return
- Highlight recent successful client implementations - Ask your network of contacts for referrals to your organization

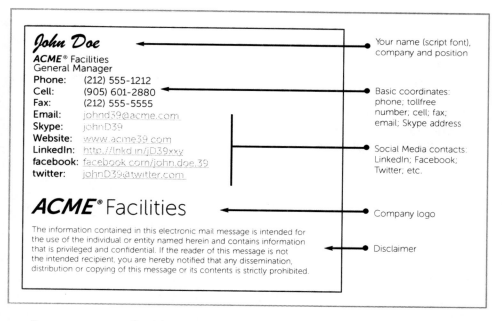

- Ensure your email address has all of your social media links embedded in the signature.
- Finally, make an extra effort to keep your sites current. Prospective customers often surf your site as a preliminary method to determine if they want to business with you or your business. Keeping your site current will speak to both your activities and recent experience

However, prospecting, like most aspects of selling, is a skill. The better armed you are with the appropriate skills, the less chance of rejection and the higher your enjoyment of this critical aspect of selling.

Depending on the type of sales product/service you represent, there are multiple ways to identify prospective clients. Examples include:

**COLD CALLING:** Possibly the most difficult, and most commonly used, ways to prospect is by cold calling. You have to make on average 20 phone calls to get through to one person and three-quarters of the time they hang up on you, blow you off to a later day, or the gatekeeper won't let through. This kind of prospecting usually requires the most amount of intrinsic self-motivation and mental strength to be able to take the rejections, brush them off, and keep on calling until you get the meeting. Then you start all over again. Here are a few simple tips to help you cold call more effectively:

- Have a well thought-out script briefly outlining your value proposition, the impact your solution or similar solutions have had on other organizations in a similar industry, and ask for a meeting. Be prepared to address common objections.
- Make the script your own and don't sound like you're reading form a script.
- Persistence beats resistance, but don't be a pest. Remember the 3 P's: **PERSISTENT, PROFESSIONAL, POLITE!**
- The best times to cold call are between 8:00 am to 10:00 am, noon to 1:00 pm, and 4:00 pm to 6:00 pm. The execs are at their desks usually at these times and the Executive Assistants usually only arrive at 9:00 am, have lunch noon to 1:00 pm, and then leave the office at 5:00 pm sharp. You'll be less likely to get a gatekeeper answering the phones and more likely to get through to the decision maker during those times.

**TRADESHOWS, CONFERENCES, AND NETWORKING EVENTS:** A favourite way to prospect is by attending targeted events. This is an opportunity to meet face to face with potential customers and other industry professionals who you can work with or stay in contact with and help each other out. You can also introduce each other to other prospects and vendors. Dress according to the dress code of the event, and don't show up with the hunger of getting new business written all over your face. Be genuine in your approach and try to get to know the people there without going into a hard sales pitch. These events are opportunities to connect with your prospects, not to sell them on the spot. If you've added enough value to the connection you've made with them, then you will have a much easier time pitching them your solution at a later date.

**DIRECT MAIL:** The power of a letter will astound you! In this day and age, where mail is scarce and email is plenty, a letter personally addressed to your prospect can bear some serious weight. Therefore sending a personalized target letter to your prospect could be a great way to get their attention if the content of that letter is right. Be sure it's targeted and personalized, rather than a generic piece of marketing. Include some industry insights or trends. To target some of the larger fish, this is sometimes the only way to get through to them, so make it count.

# LINKEDIN

The primary social media in the business community is LINKEDIN. There are some basic rules to consider when setting up your LINKEDIN account:

- Use a professional photo! Clients now peruse your site before determining whether they want to do business with you. If they login and see an unprofessional photo, their first impression of you may cause them to not bother reviewing the rest of your site.
- There are now more smart phones than desktop computers and tablets. This means prospective clients use their phones to login and review your site. Ensure you have highlighted your experience and success in your industry!
- This is the best place to have testimonials and references. Prospective clients need to know what previous clients think of your and your capabilities.
- Testimonials from leading companies and individuals strengthens your profile. Accepting anyone determines the pack you run with.
- Be cautious about agreeing to anyone linking with you.
  Many marketers use the link as a way to access your contacts!

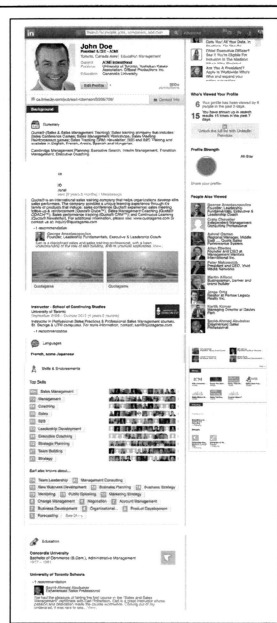

Photo - Name - Position - Education - Number of Connections

## BACKGROUND

### Summary
Summarize your background. Imagine this is the first description a prospective client reads about you.

### Experience
Start with your most recent. Ensure your experience addresses key achievements.

### Testimonials
Add in per position

### Languages
Highlight various languages

### Skills & Endorsements
Encourage colleagues to provide testimonials and agree to 'This person knows....' on their own LinkedIn accounts.

### Education
Ensure accuracy

### Interests
List - your prospect may share your interests

### Personal Details
Married - children - etc.

### Advice for Contacting you
List your primary email and cell number

### Publications
List any publications, white papers, etc.

### Honors & Awards
List any special award or recognition

### Recommendations
Encourage positive reviewers to post on your site

### Connections
The more you are connected in your industry the more business will that will flow your way

### Groups
Highlight various languages

### Following
Who you follow indicates your level of interest in your industry

# TERRITORY POTENTIAL

Let's try another equation. When we look at our individual territories, we want to know about two populations. The first is our pool of existing clients. The second is how many new potential clients (prospects) we could be selling to!

Before making the number too high, use some basic demographic 'cuts' to narrow your potential clients.  Examples of which are: Location of company, size of company (revenues; no. of employees; etc.)

According to Hootsuite, over 70% of decision makers use social media sources to obtain information prior to making a purchasing decision. As a result we are seeing a big change in traditional sales activities such as cold calling, inbound lead generation, networking, and other prospecting methods. Even the way we maintain and grow business relationships has been transformed from combining face-to-face, over the phone and email, into a whole new era of Social Media Prospecting. This is not to say that the traditional way of selling and prospecting are dead, instead we find ourselves in quite the opposite state where we are now able to enhance our phone calls, face-to-face meetings and email efforts using the insights that we gather from social media and search.

Social Media Prospecting is about reaching your target demographic at the right stage of their buying process with the right message using the right channels. Today's social media channels allow you, as a sales rep, to develop your own professional brand through various digital channels. By using your networks on LinkedIn, Twitter, Google+, and other social channels, you are able to identify potential prospects, gain intelligence into their needs and challenges, and then leverage this knowledge, your brand and social network, to provide them with valuable insights that relate to their needs. This valuable exchange of information can enable you to engage them in conversation in order to arouse their interest and get their permission to call, email, or meet with them face-to-face. Social Media prospecting provides you with a better way to uncover and establish new opportunities, and to nurture existing and developing business relationships.

Like anything, Social Media prospecting requires the right kind of process, planning, and dedication to ensure your success. Here is the process most commonly used by today's top performing social sales reps when developing their professional brands through social media and engaging their target audience to gain permission to sell to them.

## 1) Define your professional brand.

When developing your own professional brand, you need to choose how you want to define yourself. Do you want to be seen as a sales rep, as an expert in the industry that you represent or are selling into, or something else? Your answer to this question will help guide you in building your professional brand and help you determine what channels you should be using to build your reputation.

## 2) Enhance/complete your social media profiles to support your desired professional brand.

Once you establish how you wish to be perceived by your fellow peers and prospective customers, you need to take the right steps in positioning yourself accordingly through the various social media channels that are available to you. The following steps will help you get started on creating or enhancing your social media profiles to position you for the successful development of your professional brand:

> **Step 1:** Clean up ALL of your existing Social Media profiles. Remove quotes, photos, videos, and all other content that can hurst your business image.

> **Step 2:** Update your LinkedIn and other social media profiles with content that will appeal to your target audience.

> **Step 3:** Develop a content calendar to organize how you share regular content such as industry news, insightful articles, case studies and other content that is geared towards engaging your target audience based on their interests, common challenges, and more.

*See LinkedIn guidelines on previous page.*

## 3) Identify the right people in target organizations.

Like the general rule of prospecting, determine what level of decision makers you need to target and go find them through the various tools now available through social media. LinkedIn is great for this because it allows you to search for people by specific departments, titles, regions, industries, companies, and more.

## 4) Build your social networks around these people.

The best place to start is with people who you already know both socially and through past and current work experiences. Add everyone to your LinkedIn network, to Twitter, to Google+, etc. The world really is a tight knit and well connected place. Chances are that someone you know today or knew yesterday will know someone who you want to sell to or work with.

## 5) Identify the social channels your audience is active on.

With all of the different social media channels available to you, following all of them effectively is an impossible feat. In order to make the best use of your social media outlets you need to understand where your prospective customers go to search for info, to share content and ideas, to vent about their frustrations, and to get help with their challenges. If particular people who you want to prospect are regular contributors to any media channels or publications, then you want to follow those channels, join those groups, and subscribe to those publications chances are that other influential people who you will want to target are already, or soon will be, followers of those channels. You want to be where they are and you want to read up on the topics that they read up on. This will help you become an even greater expert in the industry on issues that matter to the people who you are trying to sell to.

## 6) Learn about your prospects by monitoring their activities on these channels.

What good is joining a group or following a potential prospect when you do not know why you are following them in the first place?

A big advantage that social media provides sales reps with today is that buyers are being more forthright with their needs than they were in the past. These days buyers are sending constant signals out by posting comments, sharing content, and posing questions on channels like LinkedIn, Twitter, Facebook, Google+ and more. Even their status updates might at times contain valuable information that sheds light into some of their most pressing challenges. Tools like Hootsuite,, Tweetdeck, and Google Alerts are all examples of software that can help you monitor in real time what your prospects and customers are saying online which will allow you to respond to them in a timely manner.

## 7) Offer valuable and targeted insights to engage and impress your target audience.

Now that you've defined your brand, enhanced your profiles, identified your target market and where they spend their time online, started building your network, and began learning about your prospects' challenges you are ready to start offering insights. In order to build trust and establish yourself as an expert in your field these days you need to share targeted valuable insights with your prospective customers in the form of content using the various social media channels they use to push this content to them at the right times.

*Please fill in with information from your own sales process*

Prospecting, like most aspects of selling, is a skill. The better armed you are with the appropriate skills, the less chance of rejection and the higher your enjoyment of this critical aspect of selling.

Fill in the chart below identifying where you currently find new prospects. Once identified, fill in the percentage beside the source. For example, if you get 40% of your prospects from referrals, circle REFERRALS and write 40% beside it.

| | |
|---|---|
| Social Media | _____ % |
| Trade Shows and Conferences | _____ % |
| Cold Calls | _____ % |
| Telephone Prospecting (database or directories) | _____ % |
| Advertising & Publicity lead generation | _____ % |
| Referrals | _____ % |
| Trade Publications | _____ % |
| Direct Mail (1 to many) | _____ % |
| Target Letters (1 to 1) | _____ % |
| Blue Birds (non-solicited leads) | _____ % |
| Networking Meetings and Social Contacts | _____ % |

Please take a moment to record any other types of identifying prospects that might apply to your industry:

_____

_____

_____

_____

A common analogy for prospecting is "filling the pipeline". This means that prospecting is an on-going "activity" and not an "event". If we stop prospecting for new clients to focus on existing business the time will come when there is no new business in the pipeline!

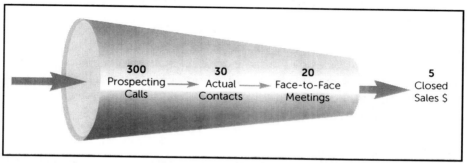

## DEVELOPING A DAILY PROSPECTING PLAN - STAGE 1

Let's say we have 20 working days/month (average) and do 15 prospecting activities/day. This will result in 300. Prospecting contacts per month. If we are fortunate, we will actually speak with 30 actual contacts (varies by marketplace) and convert 2/3 of these phone calls to 20 Face to Face Meetings. If we have a closing rate of 25% of clients we meet...we will end of with 5 additional closed sales!

# Naturally, it is a juggle – and a discipline –

to spend time prospecting while advancing existing business. Plus the lure of closing accounts (short-term) is more fun than finding new business for the future (long-term). However, any experienced salesperson will tell you that it is a lot less fun to have nothing in your Portfolio....with a quota still to achieve!

TERRITORY POTENTIAL

*For example:*

A) Total no. of prospects in your territory    =    _____

B) Total no. of customers you did
   business with in previous year    −    _____

C) Total no. of prospects left to contact    =    _____

   Divide (C) by 12 months    =    _____ /12

D) Total no. of prospects to
   contact monthly    =    _____

A) Total no. of prospects to contact daily    =    _____

So what to do? The answer lies in executing a Daily Prospecting Plan (DPP). The DPP is similar to a marketing mix. In other words, it is a multi-phased approach to sourcing new clients and business.

Once you have identified your sources, you are ready to build a prospecting list (DPP). All you need to do is structure a plan that ensures you are expending some effort, on a daily basis, to keep your pipeline filled. Please refer to the lead sources you identified on the previous pages. These sources will provide you with the best return on your prospecting efforts.

Consider the old proverb, "How do you eat an elephant?"....."One bite at a time!" Your prospecting plan abides by the same concept. Rather than trying to cram in days of prospecting when you realize your Portfolio is low, it is better to implement an hour/day on a consistent basis so that you always have a steady stream of clients in various stages of the sales cycle.

*Please see an example below of a Daily Prospecting Plan (DPP):*
As we can see from the DPP, even one hour/day will result in 110 contacts prospected over the course of a week.

Please take a minute to design your own weekly prospecting plan below: Make the daily prospecting activities as measurable as possible. For example, rather than writing "Contact some clients by telephone today" try "Telephone prospect 10 clients from my industry database".

| DAY | DATE | ACTIVITY | CONTACTED | LEFT MESSAGE | CALLED BACK |
|---|---|---|---|---|---|
| Monday | June 1 | Direct Mail 1-10 accounts from database | 3 | 7 | 2 |
| Tuesday | June 2 | Target Letter - ACME VP Operations | 1 | | |
| Wednesday | June 3 | E-mail Broadcast - 100 Dormant Clients | 100 | | 3 |
| Thursday | June 4 | Telephone Prospected - 5 referrals | 2 | 3 | 1 |
| Friday | June 5 | Advertising follow-up - 8 leads | 4 | 4 | 1 |
| Week Total | | | 110 Contacts | 14 to return | |

*NOTE: We will review how to write Target Letters, Email and Direct Mail later in the chapter.*

| DAY | DATE | ACTIVITY | CONTACTED | LEFT MESSAGE | CALLED BACK |
|---|---|---|---|---|---|
| Monday | | | | | |
| Tuesday | | | | | |
| Wednesday | | | | | |
| Thursday | | | | | |
| Friday | | | | | |
| Week Total | | | Contacts | To return calls | |

# MANAGING THE EXECUTIVE ASSISTANT

On occasion, we manage the executive assistant (or 'gatekeeper'). Pity the poor salesperson who disrespects the gatekeeper! They will have many, many months of effort trying to get past someone they have not treated properly!

Don't despair. Gatekeepers do let people pass when they believe you have clarified why their employer would want to speak with you.

**Here are a few keys to opening the gatekeeper's door:**

- Contact the client on their schedule: Mornings? Nights: Weekends? Nightline telephone line?
- Always use the client's first name.
- Always get and use the assistant's first name.
- Don't push on the first call. On the 2nd call..."Mary, this is John again. Pat and I have had a hard time reaching each other. Is there a good time for us to talk?"
- Does the assistant have access to the client's agenda? If so, book an appointment tentatively.
- Use the fax, voice mail or email to support your call!
- IF the client tries to call you back THEN you can call the assistant back and say: "Pat and I are having a hard time reaching each other. Is there a good time to connect?"
- IF the client hasn't called you back, THEN you can say "Hi Mary, this is John again, I am having a hard time reaching PAT. Is there a good time to connect?"

# If we analyze the preceding steps, we can see how they increase our success rates.

*Contact clients on their schedule: Mornings? Nights: Weekends? Nightline?*
Clients, like all of us, have their own personal schedules. Perhaps they drop off their child at daycare in the morning and then work late. Or perhaps they go the gym at lunchtime and leave at 11:45 AM. Some clients have direct phone lines during the day...or only after work hours. By tapping into the lifestyle of your clients, you will greatly increase the chances of having live conversations with them playing telephone tag. And always ask the assistant if there is a night line phone number to reach their boss.

*Use the client's first name.* With due respect to different cultural backgrounds and expectations, it is always a decision whether to use your client's first name when addressing him or her. However, for purposes of prospecting, do use the client's first name. When you ask for Mr. X or Mrs. Y, you alert the gate-keeper that you don't have a social or business relationship with his or her boss and the gatekeeper's reaction is to bar the door without further information. By asking for "John", you infer that you have an already established relationship with the boss and there is no need to "bar the door".

*Always get and use the assistant's first name.* The assistant is the first point of contact the person who determines whether you will get through to the boss or not. By using and repeating the assistant's name, you will establish a bridge between you that gets stronger with each contact. Once the bridge is built, you can then cross over it and ask for more direct assistance in speaking with his or her boss.

*Don't push on the first call.* On the second call say "Sandy, this is Chris again. Pat and I have had a hard time reaching each other. Is there a good time for us to talk?" As we have seen from point 3 – 'Getting the Assistant's Name – once you have established a bridge, you can make the gatekeeper your ally and solicit help when needed.

*Does the Assistant have access to the client's agenda?* If so, book an appointment tentatively. Some clients manage their own agendas, while others have their assistants do so. First request whether they have access to their employer's agenda (which demonstrates your respect for their status) and if so, ask if they could **TENTATIVELY** book an appointment. It is always easier to confirm than to book...so...get your name in the agenda!

*Use the Fax, Voice Mail, Text Message!* As efficient as e-mails have become, they are equally easy to discard. Receiving a communication from other sources still requires a decision before action: delegate, respond or discard? Multi-media messages reinforce who you are and why you would like to meet.

# INTRODUCTORY SCRIPT

Depending on the type of sales you are doing, you may need to introduce yourself and your company over the telephone. When this type of introductory prospecting is required, it is sometimes useful to have a basic script prepared in advance.

The value of the script is to ensure you have covered all the points you need to...and have a basic format to follow until you are more comfortable articulating your company and products/services. It goes without saying that your delivery needs to be relaxed, interactive and does not come across as though you are reading to your prospective client. In fact, many telemarketers look in a mirror while talking to monitor their own expression and presentation.

The following script gives a basic example of how an introduction could take place. Keep in mind, you need to share:

- BEST PRACTICES - LATEST TRENDS
- CRITICAL PARTNERSHIP SELLING INFORMATION

"Hello, is _____ there"

"_____ this is _____ I am with _____ Are you familiar with my company?"

If YES: "What experience have you had with _____?"

If NO: "_____ is a company that specializes in _____ We have done extensive work in your industry and many of your colleagues credit our firm with helping them _____ and improve _____ from their operations."

"My reason for calling is that I understand that _____ is experiencing _____ and might be interested in _____ through implementing the following product/services."

"What I would recommend is taking a few minutes to review your _____ needs and how _____ may help you achieve some of your _____ department goals."

Explore client needs/goals/set appointment

"_____ thanks for your time. Sounds like there are some important items for us to discuss. Lets book an appointment now and I will call a couple of days ahead of our meeting to confirm we are both still good to go."

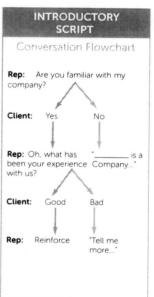

**INTRODUCTORY SCRIPT**

Conversation Flowchart

**Rep:** Are you familiar with my company?

**Client:** Yes / No

**Rep:** Oh, what has been your experience with us? / "_____ is a Company..."

**Client:** Good / Bad

**Rep:** Reinforce / "Tell me more..."

Please fill in with information from your own sales process.

Using the following script, fill in all blank spaces with information you would use to introduce your own company and product/services. Once completed, cut along perforation for later use

# HOW TO LEAVE A COMPELLING MESSAGE

When prospecting, it is typical to personally reach only 10-25% of the contacts. This means that up to 90% of your time/effort will be wasted if you don't leave a message and try to solicit a return call. In other words, there is no downside to leaving a message, but substantial downside not to. However, how you leave a message is as important as leaving the message.

Experience has shown us that clients who receive well-structured messages have a much higher likelihood of returning calls. So what exactly is a "well-structured" message? Let's take a look at the steps to leaving a message... and remember, whether it is a voice mail message or an assistant taking down the information, the steps remain the same!

- Leave a "Hook"! (Example: "I have important information for Pat on his department productivity.")
- Leave two times for the client to call back.
- Two times over two days.
- Say the number slowly and twice!
- Leave the phone number LAST.

*If we analyze the preceding steps, we can see how they increase our success rates.* Leave two times for the client to call back. Just because you are free between 3:00 and 5:00 PM today doesn't mean your client is. Leave at least two separate call back times to increase the odds of receiving the call back. And....make sure you leave times when you will be free to take the call

Two times over two days. Clients are often in full-day meetings. Make sure you leave your two call back times over two SEPARATE days. In this way, you multiply the odds you will receive a call back.

Leave a "Hook"! Accept the fact that we are all busy. When your client returns to the office or picks up messages, a quick determination will be made as to which return call gets priority. When faced with a dozen messages, all requesting a call back, your client will decide which ones can wait...or even not get a response. Your best way to receive a call back is to leave a message – the hook – that will grab your client's interest and increase the odds of a call back.

Say the number slowly and twice! We need to make it easy for our clients to return our calls! Nothing will hinder their return call faster than a number hastily left or indecipherable!

Leave the phone number LAST (slowly). Whether using voice mail, text message, or leaving a message with an assistant, always leave your number last. This ensures all previous information is listened to or read before the number is given. Plus, take your time when leaving the number. Too many call backs fail because the listener can't hear the number. Either speak your call back number slowly, or repeat it twice. After all, isn't the purpose of leaving a message to increase the odds of a return call?

Say your number slow and twice! We need to make it easy for the prospect to return our calls!

# CREATING A UNIQUE VALUE PROPOSITION (UVP) - THE 'HOOK'

One viable model to open preliminary conversations with prospects is:

- Salutation & Introduction
- When introducing yourself include: name; company and position if applicable
- Provide context for your call

A hook must demonstrate how we can help the client address their core business issues, based on the existing trigger need/objective in a manner that cannot be found else-where. Moreover, the hook must be constructed based on your understanding of what your client's key business issues are. The hook is typically a brief (2-5 sentences) description of the solution you offer.

Provide your hook right away. Give the prospect a motivation to speak with you. Your hook must be "about" their objectives and business needs... tailored to that individual (remember, different prospects care about different things). It must also demonstrate how you can uniquely (more effectively and/ or efficiently than anyone else) help them attain those objectives or satisfy their needs. Furthermore, it must demonstrate/explain a consultative nature and approach... rather than a 'sales"approach per se.

HOOK REACTION
- Request permission to proceed.
- Assess preliminary interest.
- Clarify any negative responses before trying the hook again

HOOK EXAMPLE:
"Our firm has worked with two market leaders in the industry in the past year. We have helped them both exceed their sales targets by over 25% using a new client acquisition media we have developed. Would you be free to chat this coming week?"

## HOOK PRACTICE

Use the space below to build a generic UVP for most situations in your business.

_____

_____

_____

_____

_____

_____

_____

_____

_____

_____

_____

_____

_____

_____

_____

_____

_____

_____

_____

_____

_____

_____

# HANDLING PROSPECTING OBSTACLES

So, you have successfully built a bridge with the gatekeeper and finally connected with your prospective client. As excited as you may be to finally connect, your prospect may have any number of potential objections as to why he or she is not interested in meeting you or discussing your product/services.

**DON'T DESPAIR.** This is where selling gets fun! Now you need to deal with a variety of potential roadblocks your client puts up. Here are some examples of the most prevalent and how you may respond to them to keep the sales process moving.

**IF:** The client says: "Send me a brochure"

**THEN:** Respond by saying "I would be happy to! Actually, I am meeting another client in your area next week. How about I drop the material off and if you happen to be free, I will say hello?"

**OR**

**THEN:** "I would love to. However, our product/services are quite extensive. Could I ask you a few more questions to ensure I send you the correct information?"

**IF:** The client says "Call me in a month to book a time."

**THEN:** Respond by saying "Actually, I am usually booked a month in advance. How about we book something tentative, and I will call you in a few days ahead of time to confirm?"

**IF:** The client says "I'm not interested"

**THEN:** Respond by saying "Thanks for your candor. Who would you recommend I speak with at your company who might be interested in the product/services we represent?"

**IF:** The client says "We are happy with the competition"

**THEN:** Respond by saying "I appreciate your comments. A number of our current clients felt the same way. Who would you recommend I approach to describe the new product/services we have added that distinguish us from the competition?"

**IF:** The client does not respond to any of your messages or letters.

**THEN:** Respond by sending a letter saying. "I haven't received a response to my last few letters...and I don't want to become a pest. Obviously I am contacting the wrong person in your organization. Could you please direct me to whom I should be introducing our products/services?"

# LESSONS FROM THE ROAD

Partnership selling is here to stay. Clients operate in highly competitive environments and are looking to their suppliers to provide them insight into how to use their products and services to competitive advantage.

When running a major business, I joined two of my Vice Presidents on a client meeting. The meeting was supposed to be a 'slam dunk' as our client was renewing our annual $8,000,000 contract. The reason for the slam dunk was that our firm had just won their top supplier award out of thousands of suppliers.

When we met our client, they informed us that we had provided excellent service and that in every way our service and support of our agreement was top tier. They then informed us they would not be renewing our agreement!

We were, of course, shocked and asked our client why. His answer heralded in the era of Partnership Selling. Our client said: "Actually, we have received outstanding service from your firm in almost every area of our transactions. However, you never brought us ideas. You never challenged us. You never shared industry bench mark practices. All you did was give us great service.... and that's not good enough anymore!'

Well, you can imagine how powerful this statement was and is. All of us need to understand that clients need us to so thoroughly understand their business that we need to provide them with innovative ideas and solutions...and not just great service!

P.S. It took four more months...but we re-engineered our approach and got the business!

# POP QUIZ - **PROSPECTING**

Time to test your knowledge on the preceding material with the Quota POP QUIZ! 10 questions at each POP QUIZ. Try to answer without looking at the chapter and give yourself a maximum of 2 minutes to complete the quiz.

## 1 POINT QUESTION IF CORRECT

1) To get through a 'Screen' the professional sales person must:
   a. Contact the client on your schedule
   b. Never use your client's first name
   c. Use the assistant's name when contacting the prospect
   d. None of the above

   ANSWER: ............................

2) True or False: The Introductory Script should always remain the same?
   T) True
   F ) False

   ANSWER: ............................

3) A DPP refers to:
   a. Data-Profile-Planning
   b. Drawing a Personality Profile
   c. Daily Prospecting Plan
   d. None of the above

   ANSWER: ............................

4) Key steps to leaving a message are:
   a. Two call back times
   b. Two days to reach you
   c. Leave a 'hook'
   d. All of the above

   ANSWER: ............................

5) True or False: Asking a prospect's assistant to  tentatively book an appointment is a good idea?
   T) True
   F ) False

   ANSWER: ............................

6) Examples of client's participating in the sales cycle include:
   a. Clients' review your company website
   b. Client's provide you access to other decision- makers/departments
   c. Client's arrange a product/service demonstration
   d. All of the above

   ANSWER: _____

7) True or False: A high percentage definitely means we will close business soon?
   T) True
   F) False

   ANSWER: _____

8) In business-to-business selling, the key event after Influencer Approves is?
   a. Quotation Presentation
   b. Key Decision Maker/Committee Approves
   c. Purchasing Approves
   d. None of the above

   ANSWER: _____

9) If we have successfully completed Quotation Presentation stage, our probability of closing business is?
   a. 40%
   b. 50%
   c. 60%
   d. None of the above

   ANSWER: _____

10) True or False: Relationship selling is the contemporary way to sell?
   T) True
   F ) False

   ANSWER: _____

# PROSPECTING

FINAL SCORE: _____ / 10

STAGE 2

Qualifying

PERHAPS THE MOST UNDER-VALUED AND CRITICALLY
IMPORTANT PHASE OF SELLING IS THE QUALIFYING STAGE

# *stage two*

## QUALIFYING

Perhaps the most under-valued and critically important phase of selling is the Qualifying stage. How often has a salesperson expended effort into prospecting, advancing the sales cycle, handling objections and obstacles, only to find out the client didn't have the budget or authority to make a purchasing decision?

Unfortunately, the realization that the client can't purchase happens after the time/energy/money has been expended. This is why qualifying is a critical step in the beginning stages of the sales process. By confirming, in an initial contact, that the client is qualified... and motivated... to make a purchase, the salesperson can save themselves days and months of wasted efforts.

## Potential BUYING CENTRES

Partnership Selling identifies 4 categories of potential business:
1) N = New Accounts
2) NBC = New Buying Centres
3) SBC = Same Buying Centres (Wallet Share)
4) CBC = Competitive Buying Centres

## Pre-qualified

*If we were to break down our "pipelines" into three broad stages, they would be:*
1) Our ability to source new clients (Prospecting) is ACQUISITION.
2) Our ability to source additional buying centres within existing clients is EXPANSION.
3) Our ability to close and retain clients for future business is RETENTION.

# QUALIFYING

## SALES FUNNELS
*The diagram below illustrates three different sales funnels:*

### Funnel A
Illustrates many new prospects that drop off during the sales process and end up with a small number of closed business opportunities. This is a typical approach that results in many lost opportunities and time invested without return.

### Funnel B
Illustrates those few new customers whose business does not expand during the sales process and end up with the same number of closed business opportunities as originally identified.

### Funnel C
Demonstrates how a few leads can generate additional referrals/sales cycle which ultimately results in more sales. NETWORKING EXISTING AND PRE-QUALIFIED ACCOUNTS

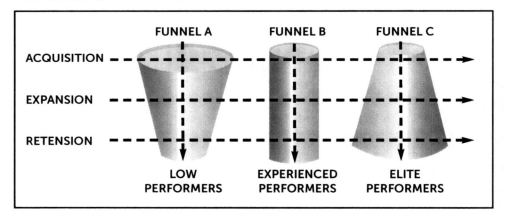

# Network Existing AND Pre-Qualified Accounts
We have learned through our research that prospecting is a continuous activity throughout the sales cycle and not just at the beginning of the cycle. In fact, successful sales people are constantly looking for ways to expand business with existing clients, and for leads to other departments or colleagues who might be interested in their products/services.

Therefore, prospecting isn't just used to acquire new business, but also to expand business within existing accounts and to source other new accounts while advancing a particular sales cycle.

Successful salespeople know that it is easier, and more efficient, to increase penetration within existing accounts than to source an entirely new account. In fact, high-performing salespeople will often have multiple sales cycles, at different stages of advancement, in the same account at the same time.

## Sales Cycle in Progress

As you can see from the two examples, the beginner salesperson expends three times the time, effort, cost and travel to cultivate three sales cycles in three different accounts, while the advanced salesperson utilizes existing account contacts and insight to advance multiple sales cycles in the same account. Ultimately the advanced sales-person can achieve much higher sales with less time and effort.

**INEXPERIENCED**
SALESPERSON

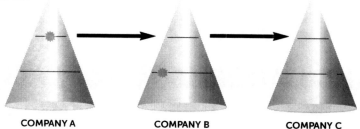

COMPANY A          COMPANY B          COMPANY C

**EXPERIENCED**
SALESPERSON

COMPANY A

✳ = Sales Cycle In Progress

As you can see from the two examples, the beginner salesperson expends three times the time, effort, cost and travel to cultivate three sales cycles in three different accounts, while the advanced salesperson utilizes existing account contacts and insight to advance multiple sales cycles in the same account. Ultimately the advanced sales-person can achieve much higher sales with less time and effort.

# B.P.O.U.T.

The B.P.O.U.T. process is an excellent way to ensure you have covered off 5 critical qualification questions.

When completed, you will have a clear indication of whether or not you want to do business with this client.

The B.P.O.U.T. process will also demonstrate to your clients that they are dealing with a professional salesperson who values their time and opportunity.

The five B.P.O.U.T. questions can be asked as a normal flow of the conversation. However, it is vitally important that you have all the questions addressed before you leave the client/conversation.

| **B** | = | Budget |
|-------|---|-----------|
| **P** | = | Potential |
| **O** | = | Ownership |
| **U** | = | Urgency |
| **T** | = | Timing |

## SUPPLEMENTAL READING

## B is for Budget.

Ultimately, your clients need to pay for the product/service. Do they have the money? Are they on a calendar (January 1st to December 31st) or fiscal (any 12 months during the year) budget? Can they pay for the purchase over two budget years (one payment on December 31st and the next on January 1st)? Whose budget will the money come from? Can any other money be found in any other budget? Does the company use accrual accounting (date of purchase versus date of payment)?

## P is for Potential.

How many employees/clients/members will be affected by this purchase, over what time period? What is the current attrition rate of employees/clients/members? How many new employees/clients/members are added each year? What level of employee will be affected by the purchase? How many units will be purchased?

## O is for Ownership.

Who will take responsibility for the purchase? Who really wants it? Is that individual the "Influencer" or the "Key Decision Maker"? Is a committee involved in the purchase? Who is on the committee? What is each individual's company and personal needs? Who will take this sale and run with it?

## U is for Urgency.

What are the consequences to your client of purchasing or not purchasing? What issues are driving the need to purchase? How have those issues manifested themselves? Why does the client need to purchase now?

## T is for Timing.

When does the client want to purchase? Why then? What happens if the timing is not a fit (see Urgency)? What makes this time better than other times? Is seasonality an issue for your client? Do players within your client's organization and your own organization have different timing issues (budget years, internal priorities, personal reasons)?

A particularly important factor is not to mistake timing for urgency. There will be occasions where your client has a high urgency, but does not need immediate timing (seasonality), or has a preference for immediate implementation....but not a high sense of urgency. This insight will be of critical importance when you update your Portfolio Management System.

# *B.P.O.U.T.* QUALIFYING PROCESS

## BUDGET

Calendar or fiscal year?
Amount available?
Willing to split among two budget years?
Access to other funds?

## POTENTIAL

Number of employees to be affected by purchase?
Over what time period?Attrition rate?
Growth rate?
No. of units purchased?

## OWNERSHIP

Key Decision Maker (KDM)?
Influencer/Driver?
Buying process?
 "Hot buttons"?
"When you and I say 'yes'... who can say 'no'?

## URGENCY

Business Issues (External, Organizational,
Functional, Performance)?
Marketplace/Industry/Competition?
Ground up?
Top down?
"What are the consequences of doing nothing?"

## TIMING

When to implement solution?
Why?
How long before approval to commence?
What could get in the way?
What are the consequences of not
implementing now?

# WRITING EMAIL BLASTS, TARGET LETTERS AND DIRECT MAIL

Part of prospecting and qualifying typically includes written communication. The primary difference between written and spoken prospecting is that when writing, you have to grab your client's attention early and present a presence that is strong enough to keep your client sufficiently interested in reading. When using written communication as an introduction, you have already pre-qualified that the company you are targeting has sufficient size/budget to be a client. Ultimately, the objective of your written communication is to secure an agreement from the prospect to meet you face-to-face.

When using written communication, you can either draft a letter that will be read by many clients (direct mail, email blast) or a letter that is specific to a single client (target letter). As a written communication doesn't have the benefits of an oral exchange, you must write a compelling enough letter that the prospect will be motivated to call you....or accept your call. E-mail broadcast is also a method for getting your message out to many prospects. Whether you use paper or electronic communication, follow the format for capturing your prospect's interest.

The following communication format provides a succinct way to capture your prospect's attention, present your company, identify the solution, and arrange a meeting. This one-way communication format follows five basic steps:

- The Situation
- The Idea
- How it Works
- The Key Benefits
- The Next Step

1) **The Situation:** In one to two sentences, immediately identify the key business issue that your clients are struggling with. This ensures quick buy-in and leads the customer to the content of your letter.

2) **The Idea:** Once your clients have recognized that you are aware of their problem, they will be interested in whether or not you have a solution. Stating the idea should also be one to two sentences only.

3) **How It Works:** This allows you to introduce your company and provide some detail on the exclusive features and benefits of your company's solution. Some detail is required but keep the description to 4 to 6 sentences maximum... remember... your intent is to get an appointment, not to all your selling in a single letter.

4) **The Key Benefits:** Before "closing" the client on a meeting, it is important to revisit the benefits the client will enjoy by utilizing your solution. This is a critical last step before asking your prospect to agree to a meeting.

5) **The Next Step:** Once you have lead your clients through their problems, your solution, the description of how your solutions work and how it will benefit them, you will finally be ready to request a meeting to "explore" whether your solution is appropriate for your client. It is equally important that the meeting be at a mutually agreeable time. You are not subservient to your clients. You are a professional bringing an important solution to their business issues.

The entire communication should NEVER exceed one page! Prospects are deluged with direct mail and target letters every day and have neither the time nor the patience to dedicate to multi-page advertising letters. You must capture your prospect's interest in the first line and then quickly build a business case as to why your letter is worth reading and considering.

In all cases, the effectiveness of your direct mail and target letters will have a strong correlation to your follow-up. Should your client receive and read your direct mail, his or her awareness of the contents and willingness to respond to your request for a meeting will dilute daily until you are a distant memory. However, should your client receive a phone call from you within 1-2 days of receiving your direct mail, the willingness to meet and your success rate at securing a meeting will go up exponentially.

On the next two pages, you will see two examples of a Direct Mail/E-mail Broadcast (one-to-many) and a Target Letter (one-to-one) using a fictitious company, TRITEC FURNITURE. The two areas that differentiate a **TARGET LETTER from a DIRECT MAIL are highlighted.**

# Writing Intro Emails that Get Responses

How often do you meet someone really interesting at an event or connect with someone you'd like to get to know or do business with on LinkedIn or Twitter? Do you have a strategy for following up with them and engaging them in future conversations?

I find email still to be one of the most effective ways to reach out to someone I've recently met or connected with online. Email is so powerful that a recent study by Exact Target found that 91% of consumers check their emails at least once per day, and over 40% of consumers check it four or more times per day as per a recent poll conducted by emailmonday.com.

*Try these 7 tips and watch your response rate grow:*

## 1) USE A MEANINGFUL SUBJECT LINE.

First thing's first, how can you hope to get a reply unless they actually open and read your email? One of the toughest parts about sending an email to someone you barely know is ensuring that they open it.

Think of your email subject line like a news headline. It should capture the recipient's interest and give them reason to open your email. Make it specific and add a personal touch to allow it to make more of an immediate impact when read.

*Here are some examples of subject lines that people have found to work for them:*

- Great meeting you at the Career Fair!
- I see you're hiring a Marketing Manager. Here's why I'd be the perfect fit!
- I thought you would find this article on (enter a topic you discussed together or their industry/company) interesting.
- Do you have 3 minutes to chat about (enter subject matter you both are interested in)?

# 2) PERSONALIZE IT WITH THEIR NAME.

NEVER use "Dear Sir / Madame" or any other generic introduction when sending an email. Personalize your message by addressing your email to a specific person and using their name. In fact I like to use their name twice, once when addressing them at the beginning of the email and once when thanking them at the end of it.

If you don't have the person's name – get it! Find it online, try calling other departments within the organization, speak with the secretary, etc. Do whatever is necessary to get their name.

If you know their name and need to find their email try calling the receptionist and say "I've been trying to email John at John@CompanyName.com regarding our discussion the other day and it keeps getting bounced back. Could you please verify if I've copied it down correctly?". If that doesn't work, try reaching out to them through LinkedIn, Google+ or other Social Media channels.

*When writing your intro email try something along these lines:*

> Hi Jessica,
> It was nice meeting you at the career fair the other day. I really enjoyed our chat about your challenges finding the right candidates! I think I can help! (Body of the email)
>
> Thank you Jessica and I look forward to your reply.

# 3) GIVE THEM AN EGO BOOST.

One of the best ways to make someone interested in you is to show them that you're interested in them first. When starting the body of your email, try to make them feel special by expressing your interest in an article they wrote or congratulating them on a recent accomplishment. If you start off by talking about specific topics that relate to them, that shows that you are genuinely interested in getting to know them and developing a relationship together.

*Here's something that works well for many of the businesses that I work with:*

> Hi Jessica,
>
> It was nice meeting you at the career fair the other day. I really enjoyed our chat about your challenges finding the right candidates! I think I can help. I read your article about the challenges that companies face when hiring sales reps and you mentioned a few things that really resonated with me. I was hoping that we could connect when you have 3 minutes to chat about the specific sales role that you're looking to fill and explore how I can help you with that challenge.

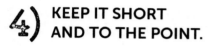

## 4) KEEP IT SHORT AND TO THE POINT.

Nobody in the business world has time to read long drawn out emails and spend time trying to decipher what the real purpose of the message is. Get to the point early on in the email and keep it simple. Make your ask known and state the potential value for the recipient early on in your message. If you want to speak with them on the phone, say so and then follow with a clear and concise value proposition letting them know how they stand to benefit from the conversation.

A proper intro email should take no longer than 45 seconds to a minute to read. After all, you will either win or loose the reader's attention in the first 10-20 seconds. If you can keep it that long, then you only have a little bit longer to get them interested enough that they'll respond.

## 5) YOU SUGGEST THE DAY AND TIME.

I often receive emails asking for a meeting or a phone conversation and asking me to suggest a day and time that's convenient for me. Contrary to popular belief, this whole approach is actually very inconvenient for someone. It forces them to look through their schedule for the entire upcoming week or two and come up with a time when they can meet. This puts the onus on the recipient and that means that they are more likely to disregard your email because they don't want the added stress of finding a time that works.

A much more effective strategy would be to present two or three possible days and times for the meeting and letting the recipient simply pick one of the options or suggest an alternative if none of the options fit their schedule. This works because rather than forcing them to look through their schedule and come up with a day and time to meet, they only need to check there availability on two or three specific times and choose one that works. This small detail makes all the difference in the world when you're trying to book a meeting or phone conversation with someone.

*Here's what it looks like in email form:*

> Hi Jessica,
> It was nice meeting you at the career fair the other day. I really enjoyed our chat about your challenges finding the right candidates! I think I can help. I read your article about the challenges that companies face when hiring sales reps and you mentioned a few things that really resonated with me. I was hoping that we could connect when you have 3 minutes to chat about the specific sales role that you're looking to fill and explore how I can help you with that challenge.
>
> How does Wednesday at 10:00 am or Thursday at 3:30 pm work for you?
>
> Thank you in advance Jessica and I look forward to your reply.
> Best regards,
> Steven

# 6) PERSISTENCE BEATS RESISTANCE.

If at first you don't succeed try, try again. That's not just a saying that your parents told you to keep you from crying when you couldn't figure out how to transition from a tricycle to a bicycle. It most definitely also applies to the business world and life in general. Since many business people are constantly busy managing everything from minor tasks to major projects, not to mention putting out fires on a daily basis, they are not always able to get through the onslaught of phone messages and emails that pile up through the day.

It may take days for some people to even get to your email. That's why the best time to send an email to a busy corporate executive is either at 8:00 am so that it's at the top of their inbox when they first check their emails in the morning, or just before noon when many execs check their emails before starting their lunch.

Sometimes no matter when you send the email it may take days for a busy executive to read and reply to them. Send your email and wait about 2 days before sending a follow up email or before calling them to see if they received and had time to read your message. Repeat this every 2 to 3 days until you get a response.

## 7) SEND IT TO EVERYONE YOU MEET.

Finally, sending an intro or thank you email to everyone you meet is a great practice. Try it and see how quickly your network grows! Whether you're a sales person looking for prospective customers, someone actively in job search mode looking for the next job opportunity, an entrepreneur looking for super talented employees, or someone interested in meeting great people and getting inspired, this is a great strategy to help you build stronger relationships with more people than ever before.

The best time to send an email to a busy corporate executive is either at 8 am or just before noon.

# TARGET LETTER

August 27

Mr. James Ashley
Vice President, Sales & Marketing
Tritec Furniture
1234 Power Avenue
Tower City, Ontario
L5B 3A1

Dear Mr. Ashley,

### THE SITUATION
COMMERCIAL REAL ESTATE magazine recently ran an article on Tritec Furniture. The article mentioned that Tritec has won the contract to supply furniture to the new City Center Tower.

### THE IDEA
This is where ACME Logistics may be of service. We are the premier supplier of logistical services to the commercial furniture industry. We can help you coordinate your inventory management and provide additional storage capacity as needed.

### HOW IT WORKS
Our logistics services have been used by some of the industry's top furniture suppliers. We can ensure your deliveries are on time, accurate and cost effective using our proprietary inventory management software – ACME ON TIME®

### THE KEY BENEFITS
By utilizing ACME Logistics you can rest assured that City Center Tower will receive their deliveries as ordered. With our assistance, Tritec Furniture will certainly be their supplier of choice for further office expansion.

### THE NEXT STEP
I would appreciate the opportunity to present our full range of capabilities to you. Please expect my call the week of May 2 to find a mutually convenient time to talk. I can be reached at 1-800-555-1111 or by e-mail at ACMELOGISTICS@sympatico.ca.

Regards,

*Pat Grey*
Account Manager
Acme Logistics

August 27

Mr. James Ashley
Vice President, Sales & Marketing
Tritec Furniture
1234 Power Avenue
Tower City, Ontario
L5B 3A1

Dear Mr. Ashley,

COMMERCIAL REAL ESTATE magazine recently ran an article
on Tritec Furniture. The article mentioned that Tritec has won the          ➨ The Situation
contract to supply furniture to the new City Center Tower.

This is where ACME Logistics may be of service.
We are the premier supplier of logistical services
to the commercial furniture industry. We can help you coordinate          ➨ The Idea
your inventory management and provide additional storage
capacity as needed.

Our logistics services have been used by some of the industry's top
furniture suppliers. We can ensure your deliveries are on time,          ➨ How it Works
accurate and cost effective using our proprietary inventory
management software – ACME ON TIME®

By utilizing ACME Logistics you can rest assured that
City Center Tower will receive their deliveries as ordered. With our          ➨ The Key Benefits
assistance, Tritec Furniture will certainly be their supplier of choice
for further office expansion.

I would appreciate the opportunity to present our full
range of capabilities to you. Please expect my call the week          ➨ The Next Step
of May 2 to find a mutually convenient time to talk.
I can be reached at 1-800-555-1111 or by e-mail at
ACMELOGISTICS@sympatico.ca.

Regards,

*Pat Grey*

# DIRECT MAIL OR E-mail

August 27

Mr. James Ashley
Vice President, Sales & Marketing
Tritec Furniture
1234 Power Avenue
Tower City, Ontario
L5B 3A1

Dear Mr. Ashley,

## THE SITUATION
Recent reports indicate that our downtown core is planning on strong growth in commercial office space rentals.

## THE IDEA
This is where ACME Logistics may be of service. We are the premier supplier of logistical services to the commercial furniture industry. We can help you coordinate your inventory management and provide additional storage capacity as needed.

## HOW IT WORKS
Our logistics services have been used by some of the industry's top Furniture suppliers. We can ensure your deliveries are on time, accurate and cost effective using our proprietary inventory management software – ACME ON TIME®

## THE KEY BENEFITS
By utilizing ACME Logistics you can rest assured that your clients will receive their deliveries as ordered and their recognize Tritec Furniture as their supplier of choice for further office expansion.

## THE NEXT STEP
I would appreciate the opportunity to present our full range of capabilities to you.  Please expect my call the week of May 2 to find a mutually convenient time to talk. I can be reached at 1-800-555-1111 or by e-mail at ACMELOGISTICS@sympatico.ca.

Regards,

*Pat Grey*
Account Manager
Acme Logistics

# LESSONS FROM THE ROAD

As a sales executive, I have sometimes seen what I coin the 'Walk of Shame'. Specifically this is the knock and walk a rep does when they come to your office to tell you they didn't land the business they have been forecasting for many months.

The walk is characterized by: eyes down; shoulder's slumped and a hesitant step. The reason for the body language is that the rep has been confidently forecasting this piece of business for many months and is embarrassed that it has somehow not come to fruition.

When we conduct our 'Mortality Analysis' (why we didn't close the business), we typically discover that the three primary reasons are:

1) Our competition was selling at a more senior level
2) The prospect had already determined who they wanted to partner with but had to show competitive quotes
3) The client didn't have access to the funds they needed to complete the transaction.

Essentially the rep has not QUALIFIED their prospect early in the process to ensure there was a legitimate opportunity to get the business. The consequence was that they spent weeks or months on a deal that never had a real chance of closing.

There is no prize in the sales world for looking good. You either closed the business or didn't. Looking busy or actively working on accounts that don't have a real possibility is a form of self deception that will always catch up to you!

Case in point. Years ago I prospected a mid-level manager at one of Canada's ministries. Closing a government deal is always exciting at the potential size of the deal is a big payoff. However, I had a sense that my prospect was just looking for ways to keep himself busy and didn't have a real intention to purchase.

I then asked this prospect one of the qualifying questions we ask from B.P.O.U.T. (U - Urgency). The question was: 'What are the consequences if your ministry doesn't purchase this service?'. His answer stopped me cold: 'Kid, there are no consequences, no one here cares!'

I'm still not sure I shook his hand as I ran out the door!

# POP QUIZ – **QUALIFYING**

Time to test your knowledge on the preceding material with the Quota POP QUIZ! 10 questions at each POP QUIZ. Try to answer without looking at the chapter and give yourself a maximum of 2 minutes to complete the quiz.

## 1 POINT QUESTION IF CORRECT

1) Successfully completing Needs Analysis stage puts us at this stage of probability:
   a. 40%
   b. 50%
   c. 60%
   d. None of the above

   ANSWER: ................................

2) True or False: B.P.O.U.T. should only be done at the end of the discussion?
   T) True
   F ) False

   ANSWER: ................................

3) The 'P' in B.P.O.U.T. refers to:
   a. Potential
   b. Population
   c. Profile
   d. None of the above

   ANSWER: ................................

4) The 'T' in B.P.O.U.T. refers to:
   a. Timing
   b. Territory
   c. Title
   d. None of the above

   ANSWER: ................................

5) True or False: Budget in B.P.O.U.T. only refers to calendar budgets?
   T) True
   F ) False

   ANSWER: ................................

6) Some steps in writing Target Letters are:
   a. Summarize the Idea
   b. Reinforce how it works
   c. State the summary
   d. None of the above

   **ANSWER:** _____

7) B.P.O.U.T. steps include:
   a. Ownership
   b. Population
   c. Timing
   d. All of the above

   **ANSWER:** _____

8) Which targets require qualification questions?
   a. New prospects
   b. Prospects using competitors product/services
   c. New buying centres within existing accounts
   d. All of the above

   **ANSWER:** _____

9) Sales funnels are composed of:
   a. Acquisition
   b. Expansion
   c. Retention
   d. All of the above

   **ANSWER:** _____

10) True or False: It is better to work three separate accounts than have 3 sales cycles within one account?
   T) True
   F ) False        **ANSWER:** _____

# QUALIFYING
**FINAL SCORE:** _____ / 10

STAGE 3

Initial Meeting

FROM THE MOMENT YOU ENTER THEIR WORK AREA, YOU ARE CREATING AN IMPRESSION

# stage three

# THE INITIAL MEETING

**MEETING YOUR CLIENT**

It has been said that 75% of communication is non-verbal. If this is true, then 75% of a first impression is what you do...not what you say. In most cases, your clients won't attend a first meeting with any bias, for or against you. They have agreed to meet and are likely interested in how your product or service can help them address a key business or personal issue. Within this context, they may be described as "neutral" to your presentation. You could say the first impression is a time to move the client from "neutral" to "positive"!

From the moment you enter their work area, you are creating an impression. Your energy level, eye contact, smile, handshake and personal confidence all have an immediate impact on your greeting. Throughout the meeting, your clients will appraise you on your integrity, honesty and sincerity.

Another key aspect of making a strong first impression is our personal confidence. **Clients need to believe in you as much as they believe in your product/service.**

*Questions they will consider include:*
"Will you be around to service me after I purchase?"
"Can I believe in what you promise?"
"Are you someone I will enjoy working with?"

# THE INITIAL MEETING

## CONFIDENCE-BUILDERS
- Making direct eye contact
- Listening more than speaking
- Letting your clients finish their thoughts
- Answering questions in a short, direct, fashion
- Matching your client's level of intensity
- Offering firm, but not crushing, handshake
- Presenting yourself professionally (make-up applied modestly, appropriate attire, personal grooming, well-mannered)
- Using appropriate humour
- Being sensitive to the client's working environment.

*So how exactly can you lose your client's confidence? Here is a list of "Confidence-Breakers" you should ensure that you are not guilty of:*

## CONFIDENCE-BREAKERS
- Avoiding eye contact
- Speaking more than listening (Remember: we have 2 ears but only 1 mouth)
- Interrupting
- Not responding to direct questions
- Being overly passive or aggressive
- Offering limp or bone-crushing handshakes
- Presenting yourself poorly (overdone make-up, inappropriate attire, body or breath odour, personal grooming, poor social manners)
- Using inappropriate humour
- Being insensitive to the client's working environment

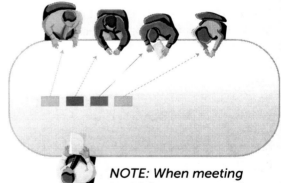

*NOTE: When meeting multiple prospects, place their business cards on the table in the same order that they are sitting across from you.*

# 5 STEPS TO A PROFESSIONAL GREETING

Confidence-Builders and Confidence-Breakers move along the same spectrum. In fact, in most cases they are opposites. Our profession requires each of us to present ourselves and our companies in the most professional way possible. Remember this quote... "When in doubt, do without." Should you ever be unsure of whether to tell a risqué joke or make an insensitive comment...do without!

- Greet your customer
- Small talk
- Present your business card
- Give before you get
- Share your meeting objectives

So what is considered a professional greeting? Let's review the basic steps:

**Greet your customer.** Smile, give a firm handshake, maintain eye contact and express your appreciation for their time.

**Small talk.** Your clients will let you know their tolerance level for chit-chat. Some clients feel it's important to discuss personal issues before getting to business....let them do so! Other clients will want to get directly to business and expect you to do the same. Follow their lead!

**Present your business card.** After sitting, pass your card over to the client, and if necessary, request one in return. his shows your client your company, full name and position and allows you the same information in return.

**Give before you get.** The best way to get information is to give information. Start the meeting with a quick overview of how you came to be in the meeting, what it is your company does and a quick history of your company

**Share your meeting objectives.** Let the clients know up front what it is you wish to achieve from this meeting, and ask them what they would like to achieve. This exchange will ensure you start from the same viewpoint.

At the end of your meeting, be sure to thank your clients for their time, confirm a next key event or meeting (as well as details you both need to accomplish in the interim) and follow up the meeting with a brief e-mail or written note recapping your discussion.

Ultimately, all things being equal, clients buy from salespeople they like. Your ability to be friendly, open, caring and interested will keep you on a level playing field.

# DECISION SPECTRUM

In simplistic terms, we evaluate our business decisions through two basic filters:

ME                                      COMPANY

What is important to our company
What is important to us

## INDIVIDUAL MOTIVATORS

Not only does the successful salesperson recognize that both individual and organization motivators come to play in the purchaser's decision, they also recognize that the weighting of each motivator will vary from buyer to buyer. Some clients will weigh their organization motivators as 80% of the decision requirement with only 20% from individual motivators. Other clients may use their individual motivator as 90% of the decision with only 10% weighting coming from organizational motivators.

Either way, remember always that purchasers consider BOTH individual and organization motivators in their decision making. Your ability to recognize how both influence the purchasing decision will have a direct impact on your closing ratio.

*The 6 primary Individual Motivators (IM) are:*

- Recognition
- Achievement
- Detail
- Power
- Affiliation
- Lifestyle

### Recognition:
The mavericks of the organization typically have Recognition IM needs. They like the spotlight and relish making something new and different happen for their organizations...particularly if they will get the credit for the decision. These risk-takers are usually quite ambitious and will look to your product or service as a way to demonstrate their drive.

### Achievement:
Clients with an Achievement IM need are often associated with Power IM needs as well. These clients are less concerned with security and more with achieving real results that benefit their organizations. Sell the outcomes to clients with Achievement IM needs. Entrepreneurs!

### Detail:
These type of clients are particularly concerned with ensuring the purchasing process is followed to the letter. They may be working in a highly bureaucratic organization, or it is their natural inclination.

### Power:
Typically found in senior line managers, clients with Power IM needs like to break new ground and be held accountable for their decisions. They also prefer to make decisions unilaterally and be recognized for their decisions.

### Affiliation:
Usually associated with a client that does not like to take risks, affiliation is the extra layer of protection offered by not being alone in the crowd. Clients with an Affiliation Motivator require the added security of knowing who else has purchased or approved the purchase of your product/service.

### Lifestyle:
Depends on where your client is in their own work/life balance. Whether they are soon to retire or part of Generation Y or X, their lifestyle often influences their business decisions.

# ORGANIZATION MOTIVATORS

Much like our Individual motivators, our organization motivators drive us towards certain decisions. Also like our individual motivators, they can sometimes be apparent, and sometimes "hidden" from obvious view.

Unlike individual motivators, our positions of responsibility in the organization typically reveal where our organization motivators lie. For instance, if you are selling your product/service to a CFO or Controller, you can be sure they have a financial motivator behind their decision-making.

This is where sensitivity and listening skills come into play. By carefully listening to and watching your clients' verbal and non-verbal responses, you will gain some insight into what motivators drive them. Even the initial telephone or face-to-face meeting provides clues to what is important to your clients. Do they concentrate on: Price? Quality? Culture? Or is their focus on: Who makes the decision? Who else has purchased? Who else agrees? Who gets the recognition?

*The three basic organization motivators are: Organization Motivators (OM)*

- Cultural
- Operational
- Financial

### Operational:

Will it do what it purports to do? Will the purchase result in quantifiable or qualifiable gains? Can the output be measured? Will the organization see a specific improvement as a result of the investment? What is the consequence of not investing in the product/service?

### Financial:

What will it cost? What is the return on investment? How long will the payback period be? Can the investment be justified financially? How much is required up front? Over time? Payment period and terms? Special discounts applicable?

### Cultural:

How it will look? Specifically, what will others in the company, marketplace or industry think of the product/ service purchase? Will it send the desired message to the viewers? Will it be seen by company executives as compatible with their vision for the organization? Will the new product/service be respected and easily adapted to? How will it augment our Human Resource Policies?

# LESSONS FROM THE ROAD

At one point in time, Canada had two national airlines. One was already a client so I approached the other with the hope to have them both as clients. On my initial meeting my prospect proceeded to chit-chat for 45 minutes. We talked about the weather, the Montreal Canadians and just about any other item you can think of.

Exasperated, I asked if we could get down to business. My prospect responded: "This is business." I knew I had just lost the account! The prospect was ascertaining: 'Do I like this person?', 'Do I trust this person?', 'What will they be like to do business with?'.

I, on the other hand, displayed my youthful impatience and desire to 'get down to business'.

Fortunately, 99% of our clients don't spend this amount of time qualifying us...but when they do...we need to respect their process and take whatever time it takes to demonstrate they are making a sound decision doing business with us!

# POP QUIZ – INITIAL MEETING

Time to test your knowledge on the preceding material with the Quota POP QUIZ! 10 questions at each POP QUIZ. Try to answer without looking at the chapter and give yourself a maximum of 2 minutes to complete the quiz.

## 1 POINT QUESTION IF CORRECT

1) Three steps in greeting clients are:
   a. Small talk
   b. Giving before you get information
   c. Thanking your client for their time
   d. All of the above

   ANSWER: ........................

2) True or False: Individual Motivators are what is important to our client's organization?
   T) True
   F ) False

   ANSWER: ........................

3) Confidence-Builders include:
   a. Crushing Handshake
   b. Appropriate Humour
   c. Not responding to direct questions
   d. None of the above

   ANSWER: ........................

4) True or False: The 'Power' Individual Motivator is commonly found in senior line managers?
   T) True
   F ) False

   ANSWER: ........................

5) True or False: Clients will let you know their tolerance level for small talk. You should follow their lead?
   T) True
   F ) False

   ANSWER: ........................

6) Confidence Breakers' include:
   a. Eye-to-eye contact
   b. Speaking less than your client
   c. Interrupting
   d. All of the above

   ANSWER: _____

7) True or False: It is best to leave your business card at the end of a meeting and not during the introduction?
   T) True
   F ) False

   ANSWER: _____

8) Individual Motivators include:
   a. Security
   b. Control
   c. Achievement
   d. All of the above

   ANSWER: _____

9) Organization Motivators include:
   a. Performance
   b. Presentation
   c. Influencing Buyers
   d. None of the above

   ANSWER: _____

10) True or False: It is a good practice to share your meeting objective with your client?
    T) True
    F ) False

    ANSWER: _____

# INITIAL MEETING

FINAL SCORE: _____ / 10

STAGE 4

Needs Analysis

Time for the 'Science of Selling'! How effectively have you mastered your sales communication and needs analysis skills?

# stage four

## NEEDS ANALYSIS

### Needs Identification Selling

Imagine yourself in a variety of different careers: Detective, Psychiatrist, Physician. Can you imagine trying to determine what the root cause of the situation is without being able to ask questions? How would you determine what happened at a crime scene without being able to interview witnesses? Or providing a medical diagnosis without being able to ask your patients what is ailing them?

Your ability to probe, analyze, and clarify information will have a direct impact on your ability to determine what ails your clients and how your product/service can best address their needs. The root of this analysis is called Needs Identification Selling. In essence, this refers to the proposition that you must first understand what it is your clients want before you are in a position to suggest what can help them address their needs.

For example, imagine two different types of car salespersons: Salesperson A greets the customer and begins their presentation by telling the client everything they think they might want in a car: "Nice to meet you sir. I notice you looking at our latest model. It has 250 horse-power, leather seats, and electric windows and package. Would you like it in red or yellow?"

Salesperson B greets the customer and begins their presentation by asking the client what they are looking for in a car: "Nice to meet you Ma'am. I notice you looking at our latest model. What is it you might be interested in having in a new car?"

# NEEDS ANALYSIS

Now imagine the person had been in a previous accident and is most interested in safety. They are looking for an anti-lock braking system (ABS), front and side airbags and side safety paneling. Which approach (A or B) do you think they would most respond to?

*For successful Needs Identification Selling, the salesperson should use the following skills:*

- Open probes – Use open-ended questions such as "Tell me more"
- Closed probes – Use "yes-no" questions such as "Is safety your number 1 priority?"
- Sensitive probes – "How many $ are your budget?"
- Understand what is a "feature" – "This model of car has front and side airbags."
- Understand what is a "benefit" – "What that means to you is our airbags will protect you from both front and side impacts."
- Acknowledge statement

    **A) Demonstrate you have heard the client by repeating the need:** 'So having both front & side airbags is essential to you when choosing a car"

    **B) Refer to the feature/benefit of your product/service:** "You will be pleased to know this particular model comes with both front & side airbags"

Summarize benefits – Before asking your clients for a commitment, it is important to summarize the key benefits they have agreed to:

_____

_____

_____

## SUMMARIZE BENEFITS

"So, we have agreed that safety is your number one priority. You also mentioned that having an automobile with both front and side airbags would provide additional safety. This model of car has both front and side airbags. You also mentioned having ABS brakes would be an important additional feature for the winding roads you frequently travel on. This model also has ABS brakes. Finally, you mentioned having a side impact bar in the car would give you additional security in the event of a crash, just like this model of car. Are there any other features you are looking for in a car?"

# PROBES

As you can see from this example, the professional salesperson knows the complete array of their products' features/ benefits, and then "probes" to identify their customers' needs before acknowledging them and explaining how their product/services can address these needs.

*Looking at your own business, identify the top 5 features/benefits of your products/services:*

**FEATURES**                    **BENEFITS**

_____         _____

_____         _____

_____         _____

_____         _____

_____         _____

*Now, create 5 examples of both "open" probes and "closed" probes to help you identify your client's needs:*

**OPEN PROBES**                 **CLOSED PROBES**

_____         _____

_____         _____

_____         _____

_____         _____

_____         _____

# SALES COMMUNICATION EXCHANGE
# ACKNOWLEDGE STATEMENTS -
# THE LONG LOST SALES SKILL!

Acknowledge statements are one of the sales professionals most important communication skills. Moving a customer from interest to need is often a reflection of whether they have recognized the importance of the feature they are scrutinizing.

A) Acknowledging the need and...

B) Addressing the need with a feature/benefit of your product/service Your analysis will identify your client's priority needs that your product/service must address.

**EXAMPLE:**
A typical sales communication exchange follows this pattern:

PROFESSIONAL GREETING
Sales Person Probes for Needs:
Customer Responds:

Sales Person identifies Need #1 and uses Acknowledging Statement

Sales Person Probes for Needs:
Customer Responds:

Sales Person identifies Need #2 and uses Acknowledging Statement

Sales Person identifies Need #3 and uses Acknowledging Statement

Sales Person Summarizes Needs/Benefits: #1, #2, #3
Customer Confirms: These as Priority Needs

Sales Person Probes for any Other Needs:
Customer Responds 'No'
Sales Person asks for Client Commitment to:
Commitment
Next Key Event
Approval

# CONDUCTING A NEEDS ANALYSIS

A suitable analogy to conducting a needs analysis is what transpires when you visit your family doctor. For physicians to diagnose what ails you, they need to ask you a series of questions to determine the symptoms and possible cause of your illness. When the questioning begins, it is important that you understand why your doctor is asking the questions so that you don't feel like the process is an interrogation. Our customers need to feel the same way.

As you begin the process of determining what business challenges your clients are facing, you need to ensure they don't feel that you are interrogating them or judging their performance. At the same time, you need to determine the root causes or development opportunities that will help your clients overcome existing performance challenges.

## Put the client at ease.

By explaining to your clients your need to ask certain questions, assuring them of confidentiality and empathizing with their discomfort with certain questions, you create the environment in which they will supply critical information to you. Your needs analysis can then focus on the crucial areas of improvement that your own product/service can address.

It is also important to recognize that HOW you conduct the needs analysis is also being closely monitored. Should you not conduct yourself professionally during this important stage, the client who referred you will receive negative feedback and, as a consequence, will not be willing to let you advance to the next stage.

By listening, responding and inquiring, the interviewee will feel you were prepared, involved and attentive.

*The keys to conducting a successful needs analysis are:*
• Give information before you request information.
• Explain to your clients why you will ask certain types of information.

# Assure your clients (and keep!) the information received confidential.

Empathize with their possible discomfort with answering certain questions (individual performance, budget criteria, performance appraisals, financial status, etc.).

Mix "open-ended" questions with "close-ended" questions so that your clients have an opportunity to elaborate and don't feel like they are being interrogated with a string of "yes", "no" answers.

Stay within the bounds of discretion (focus on only those issues that are pertinent to your own product/service benefits).

When you conduct a needs analysis, what information do you need to gather? Please take 5 minutes to write down 5 key Needs Analysis Questions that you need to ask your clients before you can present a solution:

_____

_____

_____

_____

_____

_____

_____

_____

# LESSONS FROM THE ROAD

Partnership selling demands that we provide our clients with unique insights into their business, and use of our products & services, that will provide them a competitive edge.

However, every client is different and we still need to do a needs analysis to ascertain what are the unique aspects of our client's business model. The balance point is to ask enough questions to get the insight we need....but not so many questions that our clients feel we aren't prepared and don't have any insights to offer.

I often approach a needs analysis the way my surgeon preps me. A very busy guy that sees many patients on a daily basis, he needs to make sure he clearly understands the issue, but isn't going to get bogged down in unnecessary details. Try to chit-chat with a surgeon and you will quickly be shut down!

As important as conducting a needs analysis is, keep in mind that the number of needs analysis meetings varies in accordance with the complexity of the product. Some needs analysis meetings are interwoven into the initial meeting while some require multiple meetings to determine the key needs.

A former client sold regional jets. These highly complex products sold for $10,000,000+ each and would involve aviation engineers; pilots; interior designers; and cabinet makers. It was not uncommon to have dozens of needs analysis meetings to finally confirm what the client wanted and what the quotation would be!

POP QUIZ – **NEEDS ANALYSIS**

Time to test your knowledge on the preceding material with the Quota POP QUIZ! 10 questions at each POP QUIZ. Try to answer without looking at the chapter and give yourself a maximum of 2 minutes to complete the quiz.

### 1 POINT QUESTION IF CORRECT

1) Examples of Open Probes are:
   a. "Tell me more?"
   b. "Why do you say that?"
   c. "What else would you like to happen?"
   d. All of the above

   **ANSWER:** _____

2) Acknowledging a customer's need:
   a. Demonstrates you have heard your client's needs
   b. Shows you have the perfect solution
   c. Means you are ready to 'close' them
   d. All of the above

   **ANSWER:** _____

3) True or False: It is best to summarize the benefits previously agreed to before asking for your client's Commitment?
   T) True
   F ) False

   **ANSWER:** _____

4) Steps to a successful Needs Analysis include:
   a. Mixing Open and Closed Probes
   b. Assuring Confidentiality
   c. Stay within bounds of discretion
   d. All of the above

   **ANSWER:** _____

5) True or False: Selling is one part listening and two parts speaking?
   T) True
   F ) False

   **ANSWER:** _____

6) True or False: Needs Identification Selling refer to identifying your client's needs before suggesting how your product/service can address their needs?

    T) True

    F ) False

ANSWER: ........................

7) An example of a 'Feature' is:

    a. Car has side-safety paneling

    b. Product has re-sealable pouch

    c. Furniture has 3-year warranty

    d. All of the above

ANSWER: ........................

8) An example of a 'Benefit' is:

    a. Car has airbags

    b. Product comes with tech manual

    c. Warranty ensures no-cost repair

    d. All of the above

ANSWER: ........................

9) True or False: Open Probes are questions requiring yes or no answers?

    T) True

    F ) False

ANSWER: ........................

10) True or False: You should control the discussion by asking a series of closed probes?

    T) True

    F ) False

ANSWER: ........................

# NEEDS ANALYSIS

FINAL SCORE: _____ / 10

**STAGE 5**

**Product Service Demo**

THROW SOMETHING AT THE WALL AND SEE WHAT STICKS IS <u>NOT</u> THE WAY TO GO!

*stage five*

# PRODUCT/SERVICE DEMO

**"Throw something at the wall and see what sticks."**

Unfortunately, too many of today's salespeople are still relying on this old saying. Professional selling requires us to identify our clients' needs (sometimes before they do!) and to address those needs with the appropriate product/service.

This same concept holds true for our product/service demonstrations. Although our product may have many "bells and whistles," time is limited...and so are our clients' attention spans. When they attend a product/service demo, they have specific needs they want to see your demonstration address.

## Committee Interview

In order for you to prepare your product/service demonstration, you need to speak with each planned attendee a few days before the meeting. This will provide you with insight to what their selection criteria are, what their individual motivators are, what features of your product/service you need to highlight, and what features of your product/service don't need to be addressed.

On occasion, clients may resist sharing with you the product/service details they are intent on seeing. From their viewpoint, they want to give competitors a level playing field. As admirable as this is, it could also lead to a poor experience for all parties. When you meet this resistance, let them know your intent is to spend the limited time available specifically addressing the questions each attendee has. For this reason, you need to know beforehand what their particular interests are in attending the product/service demonstration. If you continue to get resistance, let them know you certainly hope your competition has the same opportunity to identify specific needs of the attendees.

# PRODUCT/SERVICE DEMONSTRATION

The sincerity of your approach will also build the "first impression" bridge between you and your client. By professionally presenting yourself and your service, you will build a comfort level with your client that is a foundation for better rapport at the presentation phase of your sales cycle.

| COMMITTEE MEMBER | NEED #1 | NEED #2 | NEED #3 | NEED #4 | NEED #5 |
|---|---|---|---|---|---|
| Influencer **A** | ● | ● | ● | | |
| Committee Member **B** | ● | ● | | ● | |
| Committee Member **C** | ● | ● | | | ● |
| Committee Member **D** | | ● | ● | ● | |
| Committee Member **E** | ● | | ● | ● | |
| Committee Member **F** | ● | ● | | | ● |

# PRESENTATION FORMAT IBOAT

When you have completed your interviews, you are now ready to structure your presentation/demonstration. The IBOAT model provides you with a structure to ensure you are covering all bases in your product/service demonstration introductions:

*NOTE: The iboat is only the first 5 minutes of your presentation! However it ensures the rest of the presentation is on track!*

**PRESENTATION PLANNING**

✔ **I.B.O.A.T.**

✔ **Need #1** — Feature / Benefit

✔ **Need #2** — Feature / Benefit

✔ **Need #3** — Feature / Benefit

✔ **Summarize Benefits**

✔ **Close to:** a) Commitment
    b)      Action
    c) Follow Up Date

| | | |
|---|---|---|
| **I** | - | Introduce yourself, support players and attendees. |
| **B** | - | Background information. What will you be presenting? Who are you presenting to? |
| **O** | - | Objectives. What is your objective for the meeting? Review your client's objectives. |
| **A** | - | Agenda. What will the agenda be? Does it meet with your client's approval? |
| **T** | - | Time. How much time will you need? Presentation Preparation and Agenda |

After the IBOAT preparation, you will also need to prepare the format of your presentation/demonstration. Should you be sharing presentation duties with other support staff, it is very important that you do a "dry run" of the presentation: practice what you will be presenting, and in what order. Clients typically prefer to have a single "strategic orchestrator" or master of ceremonies who runs the presentation and then turns the podium over to technical experts as required.

It is also critical that you build in Q & A (question and answer) time so that your clients get a chance to "play" with the product/service. The more interactivity, the better. More on this on page 89.

A sound presentation will address all the issues your clients identified in the private meetings you had leading up to the presentation. This means you must tie in their specific business issues with specific features/benefits of your product/service. Your clients don't have the time or interest to be "feature-dumped" at your presentation. They do want to hear how your specific feature/benefits will address their specific needs.

*A standard presentation agenda:*
- Uses the IBOAT model.
- Reviews your client's business issues.
- Addresses each issue with your product/services features and benefits.
- Addresses any questions/concerns as they arise.
- Reinforced your product/services key benefits.
- Solicits feedback on your presentation and confirms next step.

# PRESENTATION PLANNING
I.B.O.A.T.
Need #1 Feature, Benefit
Need #2
Need #3

### Summarize Benefits
### Close to:
a) commitment
b) Action
c) Follow up date

Finally, this is your presentation. That means you are responsible for doing the upfront detective work on your client's needs, organizing your presenters, and then taking the lead on the presentation. It is important to know when to speak and when to snatch the micro phone away from a support person who is losing your audience.

When the pieces are put together, your product/service demonstration is a beautiful sculpture that will ensure you move to the next critical stage of your sales process

# FINAL CHALLENGES
# ROSTER SELECTION

Where in the presentation roster do you want to be? Four competitors are asked to make presentations. You are given 1st choice of 4 possible times. Which one do you choose?

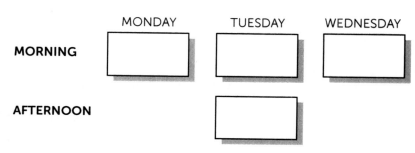

|  | MONDAY | TUESDAY | WEDNESDAY |
|---|---|---|---|
| **MORNING** | | | |
| **AFTERNOON** | | | |

## ANALYSIS

There are good reasons for any of the selections above...HOWEVER, you always want to go last if you have a friend on the committee that is telling you how your competitors are doing! This gives you the time to modify your presentation to ensure you are hitting all the committee's needs!

# Q&A

When should you build in Questions and Answers?

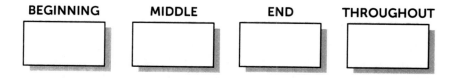

| BEGINNING | MIDDLE | END | THROUGHOUT |
|---|---|---|---|
| | | | |

## ANALYSIS

The answer is actually BOTH the END and THROUGHOUT! Telling your audience there will be a Q&A at the end will allow you the time to present without interruption. However, you will see when you have 'lost' someone and need to address their concern right away. Therefore, address both by stating: "We will have a Q&A at the end of the presentation. However, if at any point you have any concerns, please feel free to jump in and I will be happy to answer any questions!"

# PROVIDING PRESENTATION HANDOUTS

## PROS/CONS
The use of hand-outs has both positive and negative consequences. As important as the hand-out is when to give it out. What are your thoughts on the pros/cons of handouts?

| PROS | CONS |
|------|------|
| No need to take notes | Getting listener's full attention |
| Nothing gets missed | |
| Makes your coordinates easy to find | Client doesn't need to follow up with you for more info |
| | Place to keep notes if delivered early, client will skip to end/price |

| PROS | CONS |
|------|------|
| _____ | _____ |
| _____ | _____ |
| _____ | _____ |
| _____ | _____ |
| _____ | _____ |

## ANALYSIS
When providing handouts or printouts of your presentation...DO NOT include the final investment pages! Save these as separate pages you will give out at the end of your presentation...otherwise some participants will skip ahead and make a judgement on purchasing before hearing your presentation!

Finally, you need to believe personally in the amount you are quoting. Is this as good for your customer as it is for you? Is the price fair and reasonable? Will your client benefit from this purchase? If you can answer "yes" to these questions then you should feel very comfortable helping your client make this purchase...or not backing away too quickly if they decide to not move ahead or go elsewhere.

Client: _____          Date: _____

Attending:
|  | NAME | TITLE | KEY NEEDS |
|---|---|---|---|
|  | _____ | _____ | _____ |
|  | _____ | _____ | _____ |
|  | _____ | _____ | _____ |
|  | _____ | _____ | _____ |
|  | _____ | _____ | _____ |
|  | _____ | _____ | _____ |

Introduction: _____

Background: _____

Objective: _____

Agenda Topics:
    1) _____    2) _____
    3) _____    4) _____
    5) _____    6) _____
    7) _____    8) _____
    9) _____    10) _____

Timing Allotted: _____ hours

1) Primary Needs: _____
    Features: _____    Benefits: _____
    Features: _____    Benefits: _____
    Features: _____    Benefits: _____

2) Primary Needs: _____
    Features: _____    Benefits: _____
    Features: _____    Benefits: _____
    Features: _____    Benefits: _____

3) Primary Needs: _____
    Features: _____    Benefits: _____
    Features: _____    Benefits: _____
    Features: _____    Benefits: _____

Close to Commitment (Circle One): Sign P.O., Send in Proposal, Follow up Presentation

# LESSONS FROM THE ROAD

I have always been fascinated by great public speakers. Winston Churchill; Franklin Roosevelt, Paul Harvie and Bill Clinton come to mind. Their ability to capture an audience's attention and weave a story into their narrative is truly a powerful skill for any sales professional.

However, the best speakers on the planet, in my humble opinion, are televangelists. When they speak, stadiums of 70,000 are held spellbound. Their reach goes beyond the stadium as home viewers also respond to their message (and send in $ by the millions!).

When we dispassionately look at their skill sets, we see masters of communication. Their: pitch; cadence; tone; inflection; modulation; eye contact; body language; and resonant delivery are the result of decades of practice from small to large arenas.

So...if you are truly interested in improving your public speaking, try what I have been recommending to my University students for years....Go into a private television room on Sunday mornings and see if you can repeat, word for word and pitch for pitch, what your favourite televangelist is pitching on TV.

If you can, you will also have what it takes to command attention at your next public presentation!

POP QUIZ - **PRODUCT DEMO**

Time to test your knowledge on the preceding material with the Quota POP QUIZ! 10 questions at each POP QUIZ. Try to answer without looking at the chapter and give yourself a maximum of 2 minutes to complete the quiz.

### 1 POINT QUESTION IF CORRECT

1) True or False: It is important to build in Q&A time to your presentation?
   T) True
   F ) False

ANSWER: ........................

2) The 'O' in I.B.O.A.T. refers to:
   a. What outstanding issues need to be addressed?
   b. What is your/your client's meeting objectives?
   c. What is Out of Bounds to discuss at the presentation?
   d. None of the above

ANSWER: ........................

3) True or False: 'I' in I.B.O.A.T. refers to introducing yourself, colleagues, company and attendees?
   T) True
   F ) False

ANSWER: ........................

4) Presentation implementation typically includes:
   a. A 'dry run' to practice
   b. Bringing a Subject Matter Expert (SME) to address technical questions
   c. You are the strategic orchestrator that manages the information flow
   d. All of the above

ANSWER: ........................

5) True or False: Your presentation should address all the feature/benefits of all your products/services?
   T) True
   F ) False

ANSWER: ........................

6) True or False: It is best to throw as many features/benefits at our clients as possible?

        T) True

        F ) False

**ANSWER:** ........................

7) Steps in the I.B.O.A.T. process include:

        a. Institution

        b. Benefits

        c. Obvious Needs

        d. None of the above

**ANSWER:** ........................

8) True or False: When presenting to a Committee, is it best to talk with each committee member pre-presentation?

        T) True

        F ) False

**ANSWER:** ........................

9) The 'A' in I.B.O.A.T. refers to:

        a. Answer

        b. Alternative

        c. Agenda

        d. None of the above

**ANSWER:** ........................

10) A presentation agenda typically includes:

        a. Reviewing Clients business issues

        b. Address questions as they arise

        c. Solicit feedback post-presentation

        d. All of the above

**ANSWER:** ........................

# PRODUCT DEMO

**FINAL SCORE:** _____ / 10

# STAGE 6

## Quotation Presentation

A QUOTATION IS AN OUTCOME OF THE WORK AND EFFORT YOU BOTH HAVE PUT INTO MOVING THE PROCESS ALONG

# QUOTATION

A quotation is an outcome of the work and effort you both have put into moving the process along. It is rare for clients to back away after they have put as much effort into the sales process as they have.

During the quotation presentation, it is wise to wait for your client to ask about the cost. This small technique demonstrates that your client is now thinking of what it will take to close the deal. There is no better "cue" for presenting your quotation than having a client ask what the investment will be.

However, the sale could still be lost if this is not handled properly. Besides the actual price, there are seven basic rules for presenting a quotation:

*Seven basic rules for presenting a quotation:*
1) Make sure your numbers add up! Double and triple-check your calculations.
2) Ensure all names and titles are spelled correctly! Sloppiness at this stage indicates the quotation could also be incorrect.
3) Review with your Manager before presenting.
4) Review with the Influencer before allowing the quote to be sent to committee/KDM/purchasing.
5) Don't forget applicable/previously agreed-to discounts. Clients don't forget previous promises.
6) Close your client to a commitment! Either sign then, or confirm when you can pick up the signed quotation. Put a time limit on how long the quote is good for.
7) Be prepared for some last minute bargaining! Some clients use the quote as a last-chance to extract concessions. It is always a good idea to have something to offer if pressed...or to have a previously determined bottom line you won't go past.

We often presume our Quotations will be read by the person we have been interacting with. However, the quotation may also be shared with other members of a buying committee or with a final decision maker. Therefore we need to follow some basic points when structuring our presentation:

Keep the quotation to a maximum of 2-3 pages! All other information can be addressed in the ADDENDUM. No need to force a prospect to read 20 pages when the 'specs' can be referred to in the addendum

## CONTEXT:
Add 1-2 paragraphs targeted towards a new decision maker you haven't met. Explain why your firm has been asked to quote and what key issue your quotation will address

## SOLUTION:
Clients don't buy products or services. They buy 'Outcomes'...or what your product or service will do for them. Describe that outcome here!

## BENEFITS:
ALWAYS describe the expected outcomes or benefits BEFORE asking the client for a commitment!

## INVESTMENT:
Never describe 'Cost'. Alway refer to 'Investment'. After all, your client isn't throwing money away, they are investing in an outcome!

## EXPIRY DATE:
Should accompany every quotation! Not only does this provide some pressure on receiving a decision, but THINGS CHANGE! Protect yourself against future cost fluctuations.

## COMMITMENT:
Every quotation must have a place where your client can (immediately if possible) give you their commitment!

| | |
|---|---|
| **Context:** | Why this quote is good for your client and what it will do for them |
| **Solution:** | How your product/service will work |
| **Benefits:** | What benefits the client should expect to see |
| **Investment:** | Cost per unit/implementation |
| **Expiry Date:** | Day the quotation expires |
| **Commitment:** | Signature/P.O.#/Some place the client signs to commit themselves |

Why we should get a second opinion on important proposals?

### Jumbled Words

Aoccdrnig to rseearch at Cmabrigde Uinervtisy, it deosn't mttaer in waht oredr the ltteers in a wrod are, the olny iprmoatnt tihng is taht the frist and lsat ltteer be at the rghit pclae.

The rset can be a total mses and you can sitll raed it wouthit porbelm. Tihs is bcuseae the huamn mnid deos not raed ervey lteter by istlef, but the wrod as a wlohe.

# USE YOUR ADDENDUM

NOTE: Keep your quotation on point. Nothing can be more distracting to the flow of your quotation than pages and pages of product specifications. Move unnecessary information (Company Profile, Product Specifications; Personnel Bios) to the Addendum. This will allow your client to follow the 'flow' of your quotation and still find the details of your quote in the addendum if interested.

# RFP-RFQ-RFS

To do or not to do? Should you be in the business of receiving/ responding to RFQ (Request for Quotation), etc, you know how much time is required to fill it in. When you are concerned that the client already has a preference of who they would like to work with - engage them. Ask them if you have a legitimate opportunity to

win the business and that you will certainly fill in the RFQ if they say you do. Even if you don't get the bid...they now know who you are and you will have a better chance next time around.

# LESSONS FROM THE ROAD

My students at the University of Toronto frequently asked me three questions:

**A)** How many options should I present my clients?
**B)** Should I respond to every RFP?
**C)** Is there ever a time we quote but don't want the business?

*My responses are:*

**A)** The fewer the options the better. If we really do a comprehensive needs analysis then the quotation should not have multiple options! The higher our understanding of what specifically it is our client needs, the lower the number of options presented to them. There are, of course, situations where the client needs to review various options...but do your best to minimize them!

**B)** RFP (Requests for Proposal) are one of those 'darned if you do, darned if you don't' situations. Even the most basic RFP can take days to complete...and often with little insight into who gets chosen and why. In many cases, companies already know who they want to do business with but their internal purchasing process insists on going to tender. The result is a number of firms spend days on completing an RFP they had no chance to win. I actually had a past client photocopy our catalogue and make it the basis for tender...needless to say...we won the bid! Our suggestion is to contact the RFP authority and probe how real the bid is. They will, of course, tell you everyone has a chance at winning the bid. Reiterate that you will send in your RFP if they feel you have a fair chance. Even if you don't win this round...they will know who you are the next!

**C)** One of our key clients privately let us know that they had already chosen who they wanted to do business with and it wasn't us. However, they needed us to provide a quotation to make it look like they had reviewed competitive quotes. This put our firm in the difficult situation of bidding on a piece of business we knew we weren't going to get. The solution? We put in a 'stink' bid. Our competitor was bidding at $1,200,000 so we bid at $600,000. We crossed our fingers and hoped to NOT win! The result was that our price was so low it forced our competitor to shave off all their profit from the bid. This isn't a strategy you want to employ very often, but every now and then....

# POP QUIZ – QUOTATION

Time to test your knowledge on the preceding material with the Quota POP QUIZ! 10 questions at each POP QUIZ. Try to answer without looking at the chapter and give yourself a maximum of 2 minutes to complete the quiz.

### 1 POINT QUESTION IF CORRECT

1) True or False: It is best to ignore previously offered discounts when submitting the final quotation?
   - T) True
   - F ) False

   ANSWER: _____

2) True or False: When preparing the quotation, it is wise to put your best price in on the first submission?
   - T) True
   - F ) False

   ANSWER: _____

3) Questions to ask when preparing a quotation are:
   - a. Is the price fair/reasonable?
   - b. Will my client benefit from this purchase?
   - c. Is this as good for my client as it is for me?
   - d. All of the above

   ANSWER: _____

4) True or False: You should know your bottom line when entering into a negotiation?
   - T) True
   - F ) False

   ANSWER: _____

5) True or False: Clients that have invested as much work into the quotation as you are more likely to say no?
   - T) True
   - F ) False

   ANSWER: _____

6) True or False: It is best to throw as many features/benefits at our clients as possible?

    T) True

    F ) False

ANSWER: _____

7) Steps in the I.B.O.A.T. process include:

    a. Institution

    b. Benefits

    c. Obvious Needs

    d. None of the above

ANSWER: _____

8) True or False: When presenting to a Committee, is it best to talk with each committee member pre-presentation?

    T) True

    F ) False

ANSWER: _____

9) The 'A' in I.B.O.A.T. refers to:

    a. Answer

    b. Alternative

    c. Agenda

    d. None of the above

ANSWER: _____

10) A presentation agenda typically includes:

    a. Reviewing Clients business issues

    b. Address questions as they arise

    c. Solicit feedback post-presentation

    d. All of the above

ANSWER: _____

# QUOTATION

FINAL SCORE: _____ / 10

NOTES:

STAGE 7

**Influencer Approves**

THE INFLUENCER IS SOMEONE WHO NEEDS TO BE INVOLVED WITH THE PURCHASE PROCESS, EVEN THOUGH HE OR SHE IS NOT THE FINAL DECISION-MAKER

# stage seven

## INFLUENCER APPROVES

So, what is an "Influencer"? The influencer is someone who needs to be involved with the purchase process, even though he or she is not the final decision-maker. For our purposes, we refer to the final decision-maker as the Key Decision Maker or KDM.

The influencer is often someone in your client organization who will be impacted by the purchase and can be favorably inclined or negatively inclined to use it. Often the influencer is someone who strongly wants your product/ service and needs others to see the same benefits before it can be purchased. For this reason, the influencer will often become your internal partner and will direct you to whomever he or she believes needs to be part of the final decision-making.

As we often meet with the influencer(s) over a period of time, we have the advantage of gauging their emotional state of mind in regards to purchasing our product/service. In these situations, the DECISION LADDER can be a useful way to analyze where we are and where we need to be.

Recognizing our clients' emotional state of mind... and moving them up the ladder, will ultimately move them to the 'Enthusiastic' stage where they are eager to purchase your product/service!

# INFLUENCER APPROVES

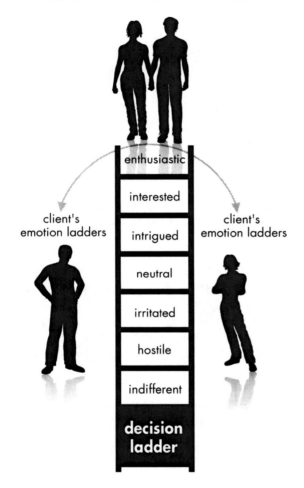

**NOTE #1**
Wait for your client to ask about price!

**NOTE #2**
When your clients begin discussing how to use your product - be a NINJA!

## POSITIVE INFLUENCE
Enthusiastic
Interested
Intrigued

## NEGATIVE INFLUENCE
Irritated
Hostile
Indifferent

# BUYING SIGNALS

Clients will often present you with "cues" that identify their willingness to close the deal. Examples are when clients:

- need you to take charge and make the decision for them
- want a final concession before committing
- need other examples of successful purchases
- want to feel that they are making the decision themselves
- would like a final reassurance that the purchase will be well-received
- needs to know that others in the organization are supportive of the decision
- are relying on your relationship and the trust built up during the sales process
- needs reassurance that their contribution/decision will be recognized

# SECURING A COMMITMENT

As we have learned, securing a commitment is less an event than an activity. If we have successfully involved our clients in moving through each of the key events of our sales cycle, closing is a natural next step in our relationship. However, even the most dedicated customer knows that confirming the order is a final step that commits both parties to the relationship.

For this reason, the salesperson needs to be adept at a variety of "closes" to use with a variety of buying styles. Some of these closing techniques are more suited to a particular purchaser's motivators than others. Depending on your own client's motivators, there will be times you need to be comfortable utilizing a more appropriate close for the opportunity presented.

# CLOSING STYLES

99% of client closing opportunities are illustrated by these basic examples. Therefore, we want to have a specific close for a specific type of opportunity. Here are 6 different, but equally effective, closing styles you may want to employ:

## 6 CLOSING STYLES

1) Direct
2) Alternative
3) Narrative
4) Physical/Assumptive
5) Stepped
6) Supported

## 1) **DIRECT** CLOSE

The direct close is the most simple...and sometimes the most difficult closing technique in your repertoire. A direct close is direct, simple, to the point, and close-ended.

> "I would like your order"
> "Please sign here to order"
> "Do I have your agreement?"

## 2) **ALTERNATIVE** CLOSE

The alternative close is a softer version of the direct close. The alternative close gives your buyer a choice between two alternatives. This close still presumes clients will agree to purchase, however, it gives them some control over other variables such as delivery dates or quantities.

> "Would you like it to arrive on Monday or Tuesday?"
> "Would you prefer to have 40 or 50 cases of product?"
> "Do you want me to give an immediate discount on this order, or add it to the annual rebate?"

## 3) **NARRATIVE** CLOSE

The narrative close is about 'painting a word picture'. You want to describe for the client how positive their decision will be seen by others. Explain how it will be seen a ground-breaking or unique and that you will want their permission to publicize their terrific insights using the company newsletter or attending a V.I.P. meeting at your company. Narrative close must address your client's need for recognition by highlighting the expected 'press' they will receive for taking this step!

# 4) PHYSICAL/ASSUMPTIVE CLOSE

The physical close is often used in fast-paced environments (e.g.grocery, packaged goods, wholesalers) but can be equally effective in boardroom settings. When the quotation has been presented and all questions asked and answered, it is time to close. A physical close could be as simple as passing over a pen to sign, or walking over to a purchase sheet (and hoping your client is following you!). Assumptive close is closely related to the Physical close as both rely on your showing your client your belief they will sign. Whether offering a pen to sign or using an assumptive approach in the contract signing, you are letting the client know you expect them to fulfill their obligation to close the deal! Either way, your expression of confidence and ability to let the silence do the work for you can be very effective.

# 5) STEPPED CLOSE

The stepped close refers to either a series of small commitments that result in a large commitment or a process of steps that conclude the sale. For instance, rather than asking your client to commit to one large purchase, you instead suggest trying the product/service for a trial period. Once the trial is over, you then suggest committing to a small amount first to ensure satisfaction. Finally, you suggest setting up a blanket purchase order (P.O.) so that clients can order as they like without filling in a new P.O. each time they purchase.

In this way, clients feel that they are in control of the process and don't need to make a significant decision before moving ahead. The stepped close is one of the most effective closes as the clients never feel they are making a signifi- cant decision, rather that they are simply working in partnership with you to support their organization's needs.

# 6) SUPPORTED CLOSE

Many clients need to know they are making a "safe" decision. By safe, we mean a decision that won't cause them or their company to regret making the purchase. This is where a supported close is best used. Letters of reference, proof sources (e.g. newspaper clippings, trade magazines, and client testimonials) are all useful at this stage of your sale.

Internal references are also essential to a strong supported close. Reminding your client of the various other contacts within the company that have approved the purchase will help put his/her mind at ease. After all, if everyone else in the company thinks this is a good purchase, the client can't be singled out later for an error in judgment. Ultimately, the supported close ensures that your client can rest easy and won't be held individually responsible for the purchase decision.

# TAILORING THE CLOSE TO THE BUYING STYLE

As we discussed earlier, there are 6 core Individual Motivators and 3 core Organizational Motivators. Keeping these motivators in mind, here are some suggested closing skills most appropriate to the buying style of our clients:

| INDIVIDUAL MOTIVATORS (IM) | PREFERRED CLOSING STYLE(S) |
|---|---|
| • Recognition | • Narrative |
| • Achievement | • Direct/Alternative |
| • Detail | • Stepped |
| • Power | • Direct/Physical/Assumptive |
| • Affiliation | • Supported |
| • Lifestyle | • Narrative |
| **ORGANIZATION MOTIVATORS (OM)** | |
| • Cultural | • Narrative |
| • Operations | • Supported |
| • Financial | • Stepped |

Ultimately, your ability to close will be a combination of all the factors involved in the entire sales process. These factors include your initial contact, the quality of your analysis and presentation, your sensitivity to the client's internal process, and the value of your proposition. However, more than one sale has been lost when the salesperson employed the incorrect close after a successful analysis. Your ability to identify your client's individual and organization motivators and then to select the appropriate close will ensure your successful close of business!

# LESSONS FROM THE ROAD

After running multiple organizations as either GM or President, I frequently meet former employees in airports or conferences. To a person, they thank me for teaching them the Customer Style analysis we covered in this section. They tell me that it has provided them a fantastic tool that has contributed to their own sales success.

Naturally, I am gratified to hear the feedback and see how the customer analysis (Individual & Organization Motivators) and preferred Closing Styles has been so impactful on so many.

The root of this practice came from my athletic background. As a former fighter, I would analyze my opponent's fighting style (aggressive, counter-puncher; defensive; elusive; etc.) and determine which style worked best against their particular style. In short order, I had a note pad that listed each fighter on our competitive circuit and which style worked best against them. Word got out and I was frequently approached by other fighters who would ask me which style to use against one of their opponents!

What it came down to was 'sensitivity'. The closer I watched each opponent, the more information I would glean.

Fast forward to my post-athletic career and I discovered the same held true for clients. The more I watched, and listened, to each client, the more information I would glean.

When we combine our analysis with the preferred closing style, we end up with a winning combination of sensitivity and skill to advance our sales process!

# POP QUIZ – INFLUENCER APPROVES

Time to test your knowledge on the preceding material with the Quota POP QUIZ! 10 questions at each POP QUIZ. Try to answer without looking at the chapter and give yourself a maximum of 2 minutes to complete the quiz.

## 1 POINT QUESTION IF CORRECT

1) Examples of Direct Closes include:
   a. 'Please think about it on the weekend'
   b. Would you like that on Monday or Tuesday?'
   c. 'Sign here, please'
   d. None of the above

   **ANSWER:** _____

2) True or False: A series of small commitments that result in a large commitment is a 'Stepped' Close?
   T) True
   F ) False

   **ANSWER:** _____

3) If our client has an 'Affiliation' need we are best to use this type of close:
   a. Supported
   b. Physical
   c. Direct
   d. None of the above

   **ANSWER:** _____

4) If our client has a 'Recognition' need we are best to use this type of close:
   a. Supported
   b. Suggestive
   c. Narrative
   d. None of the above

   **ANSWER:**

5) True or False: Lifestyle Individual Motivators are only found in young clients?
   T) True
   F ) False

   **ANSWER:** _____

6) True or False: Definition of an influencer is someone who is involved in the sales process but not the final decision-maker?

    T) True

    F ) False

                                   **ANSWER:** _____

7) Detail Motivators are often found in:

    a. Engineering

    b. Accounting

    c. Production

    d. All of the above

                                     **ANSWER:** _____

8) Various Closing Skills include:

    a. Begging

    b. Crying

    c. Alternative choices

    d. None of the above

                                     **ANSWER:** _____

9) This closing style is best used with clients with a Recognition Individual Motivator:

    a. Supported

    b. Narrative

    c. Stepped

    d. All of the above

                                   **ANSWER:** _____

10) True or False: 'Physical' close refers to a physical action leading to a commitment?

    T) True

    F ) False

                                     **ANSWER:** _____

# INFLUENCER APPROVES

                                **FINAL SCORE:** _____ / 10

STAGE 8

**KDM Committee
Approves**

"THE HARDER I WORK... THE LUCKIER I GET!"
SAMUEL GOLDWYN

# stage eight

## KEY DECISION MAKER/ COMMITEE APPROVES

## TARGET YOUR AUDIENCE

Depending on the size or context of your order, internal committees are frequently mandated to source and review competitive bids and make a final determination of who will get the business. Typically, the committees are either cross-functional (across a variety of affected departments) or comprised of one department's managers.

On occasion, the final Key Decision-Maker (KDM) is part of the reviewing committee, or is outside the committee and gives final approval to the committee's recommendation. Your job, if you have the opportunity, is to access both the KDM and as many members of the committee as you can before your presentation to them.

## PURCHASING CRITERIA

Buying committee's frequently evaluate a variety of vendors on select purchasing criteria. This means you will need to address the features and benefits your clients are looking for and weave competitive selling into your presentation at the same time.

*Critical factors on which your clients will appraise you and your competitors are:*
- Reliability of offering (Does it do what you say it will do?)
- Relevance (Is it the right application for the need identified?)
- Quality (Will it continue to do what you say it will do?)
- Price (How does the cost compare with the market?)
- Service (Will you be there to ensure a successful implementation/delivery?)
- Flexibility (Are you flexible in altering your product/service if demands are revised?)
- Relationship of our clients and competitors (is there a prior relationship?)

# KEY DECISION MAKER APPROVES

You might also notice that price is not listed above as the number one factor that clients appraise. This is not an error! Research has demonstrated repeatedly that clients value reliability, quality and service as being equal to or more important than price. Dropping your price in a competitive encounter can actually back-fire, as it presents an image of reduced quality!

## QUESTION

What is the best way to determine client's purchasing criteria?

**ANSWER:**
Ask them what their purchasing criteria are.

# COMPETITIVE SELLING PRACTICES

Competition is a fact of life.  In fact, the presence of a competitor is a sign that your client is serious about purchasing. While you should be pleased that your client is serious, a competitor's presence also signals the need for extra vigilence in all aspects of your presentation, proposal and follow up.

Once you have determined the price and quality levels you will present to your client, you now need to add in a new dimension of analysis due to the competitor's presence.  This analysis will guide you on how to create a proposal that highlights your product/service strengths...and your competitor's weaknesses.  Some ground rules on competitive selling:

- NEVER talk badly about your competitors.
- Gather as much information about your competitors as you can and create a competitive database you can refer to on     future sales.
- Encourage your clients to clarify what criteria they are using to evaluate competitive bids.
- Make your clients comfortable that they are evaluating different sources of suppliers. The more comfortable they are, the more information you will receive

*In order to position yourself against a competitive bid, you first must identify the following:*

# YOUR EXCLUSIVE STRENGTHS

What are the unique strengths your organization or product/services have compared to the competition? An exclusive strength would be something you do uniquely or better than your competitor. For example, perhaps your firm offers a 24/7 Service Line post-purchase and your competitor's does not. Or, perhaps you have free shipping and delivery and your competitor charges for these services. By listing your exclusive strengths, you can prepare to highlight why your client is better off purchasing from you than from your competitor.

What are your company's Exclusive Strengths?  Please take 5 minutes to write down 5 key areas where your product/services outshine your competition:

## QUESTION
How do you respond to a client that asks you ...
"Do you do work for my competitor?"

**ANSWER:**
"All our work is confidential – Just as what we do with you stays absolutely confidential."

# COMPETITOR'S STRENGTHS

## YOUR COMPETITOR'S EXCLUSIVE STRENGTHS
Conversely, your competition may have unique services/offerings that your firm does not. As the famous Author of the ART OF WAR, Master SunTzu, taught us, knowing ourselves is only half our battle. By knowing both ourselves and our competition, we are in a much stronger position to win the sale.

*"Know the other and know yourself:*
*One hundred challenges without danger;*
*Know not the other and yet know yourself:*
*One triumph and one defeat;*
*Know not the other and know not yourself:*
*Every challenge is certain peril."*

*Master Sun Tzu*

# COMPETITIVE SELLING

What are the unique strengths that your competitor's organization or product/ services have compared to your company? By listing their exclusive strengths, you can prepare to minimize their offering, or reinforce your strengths and why your client is better off purchasing from you than from your competitor.

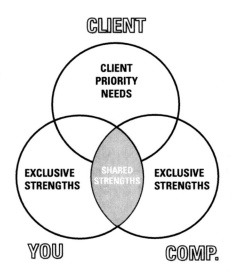

*What are your competitor's Exclusive Strengths? Please take 5 minutes to write down 5 key areas where their product/ services outshine your company.*

# SHARED STRENGTHS

Just as both you and your competitor have Exclusive Strengths, you likely will also have common strengths. Examples might include that you both have 24/7 service lines; you both provide similar delivery charges, or you both have local service technicians available for site visits. In cases where these features are important to your client, you need to highlight them.

However, there is no need to dwell on these particular shared strengths when you can instead focus on other exclusive strengths you know your competitor does not have. Ultimately, your client will transpose their needs on the product/service features/benefits you can offer. By addressing all of their concerns with both your shared and exclusive strengths, you will build a powerful case for their selecting your company to do business with!

*What are the Shared Strengths you and your competitor both offer? Please take 5 minutes to write down 5 key strengths both companies offer.*

# LESSONS FROM THE ROAD

Closing a sale is like building a partnership. There are a series of steps required in any partnership that build trust and respect. Most successful partnerships were not consummated in a weekend! Rather, they were the result of multiple occasions of working together and understanding how the other partner behaved and managed in both positive and negative situations.

When a client tells me that their sales people aren't effective 'closers', what I hear is that they aren't effective 'partnership builders'. The reality is that the close is one of the easiest stages of the sales process....if you have built up a mutually respectful partnership.

So, how do we do this? The answer is honesty and integrity. When your client has seen you on multiple occasions and each time you have acted with integrity, you are building the bridge for future success. If you ever behave inappropriately (didn't provide the discount you promised, didn't deliver on a commitment, misrepresented yourself or an outcome) don't expect your client to choose you as a future partner.

My business experience has taught me that you may not win every bid... but you will get another opportunity if your prospect respected your honesty. And, then you will realize it wasn't your ability to close but your ability to partner that won the day.

# POP QUIZ - KDM APPROVES

Time to test your knowledge on the preceding material with the Quota POP QUIZ! 10 questions at each POP QUIZ. Try to answer without looking at the chapter and give yourself a maximum of 2 minutes to complete the quiz.

## 1 POINT QUESTION IF CORRECT

1) True or False: It is best to avoid any committee member that doesn't want to speak with you?

       T) True

       F ) False

                     **ANSWER:** ......................

2) An 'Exclusive Strength' in competitive selling is:

       a. A capability both you and your competitor share?

       b. A capability neither you nor your competitor has?

       c. A unique capability only you or the competitor has?

       d. None of the above

                     **ANSWER:** ......................

3) True or False: 'Price' is always the number one criteria clients use to decide on a purchase?

       T) True

       F ) False

                     **ANSWER:** ......................

4) Master Sun Tzu wrote:

       a. 'On war'

       b. Confusian Wisdom

       c. The Art of War

       d. All of the above

                     **ANSWER:** ......................

5) True or False: Clients sourcing competitive quotes indicate their serious intent to purchase?

       T) True

       F ) False

                     **ANSWER:** ......................

6) True or False: The final KDM is always a member of the review committee?

    T) True

    F ) False

                                    **ANSWER:** _____

7) Clients purchasing criteria may include:

    a. Reliability

    b. Service

    c. Relevance

    d. All of the above

                                      **ANSWER:** _____

8) True or False: It is best to not involve the influencer when you contact other committee members?

    T) True

    F ) False

                                      **ANSWER:** _____

9) Clients purchasing criteria may also include:

    a. Quality

    b. Price

    c. Flexibility

    d. All of the above

                                      **ANSWER:** _____

10) When selling against the competition, you should:

    a. Speak badly about their service levels

    b. Create a competitive 'data' base

    c. Berate your client for considering another supplier

    d. None of the above

                                      **ANSWER:** _____

# KDM APPROVES

FINAL SCORE: _____ / 10

STAGE 9

Purchasing
Approves
P.O. Sent

Many sales have been lost at this stage of the sales process. Purchasing may override the KDM for budget reasons

# stage nine

## PURCHASING APPROVES/P.O. SENT

Many sales have been lost at this stage of the sales process. Even when you have secured the Key Decision Maker's commitment, Purchasing may override the KDM for larger, budget reasons.

So what to do? The answer lies in understanding your client's buying cycle...and in knowing whether Purchasing has the authority to halt the process. If you determine they do, then you need to involve them early in the cycle and keep them informed as you progress through the key events.

Another important consideration is that the purchasing department frequently has its own cost containment objectives. When negotiating with your client on price, it is always a good idea to save a little margin that you can pass on to Purchasing if needed. This "negotiation" with Purchasing allows them to demonstrate to the line managers how they have "saved" them budget dollars and contributes to a savings "pool" that they have achieved for their company... and may potentially earn bonus on!

Please follow the steps in the order presented below.

**1)** Solicit KDM support
**2)** Review all steps taken to date
**3)** Time to negotiate

# PURCHASING APPROVES

## HANDLING PURCHASING OBSTACLES

When Purchasing does present an obstacle, it is important to treat the department with the respect they feel they deserve. Becoming argumentative or dismissing their interference is a quick route to a lost sale. There are a few strategies that can get your sales back on track quickly.

### THEY ARE:

**Solicit KDM support:**

Once the line operation (KDM or committee) has approved the purchase, they can usually persuade Purchasing to move ahead. If they are not senior enough, you will need to solicit their agreement for a meeting (KDM, you and the KDM's manager) to meet and agree to the purchase. This method will move you up the chain of command to a level that is senior to the Purchasing department.

**Review all steps taken to date:**

If Purchasing is not supporting your sale, it could be because they have been kept out of the loop. A solution could be to put the sale on hold while you make a presentation to Purchasing on your product/service, pricing, and specific benefits to your client's company. This will frequently release the obstacle and garner Purchasing support.

**Time to negotiate:**

Understanding that Purchasing is interested in supporting their company and helping it contain costs give you an opportunity to address these two important needs. By involving them in the final negotiation, you will address any potential concerns immediately and solicit their passive support of your proposal.

# NEGOTIATING

An entire course could be done on negotiating...and there are many that do! However, there are a few basic steps to an effective negotiation anyone can learn. These steps do require an interest in negotiating a solution that both parties are comfortable with. When they are used, you will discover that you have set the stage for a long-term client relationship based on mutual respect and mutual benefit:

**STEP ONE:** Define current situation in terms of what is needed and what has been offered.

**STEP TWO:** Review all steps personnel met to date.

**STEP THREE:** Review benefits of your solution and solicit the client's agreement to the benefits. Confirm existing gap between what is needed/offered and the client's current restrictions (What they can and cannot do)

**STEP FOUR:** Reinforce your interest in finding a solution that is a win for both parties.

**STEP FIVE:** Invite your client to suggest solutions. If none are forthcoming, offer alternatives yourself. Tie in discount concessions to future purchases.

**STEP SIX:** Confirm solution and thank clients for their interest in also finding a win/win solution.

| Cost | Your Proposal | | Client Wants |
|---|---|---|---|
| $ 2,000/yr. | 2% rebate | | 4% rebate |
| $450 | 3 free service calls | | 6 free service calls |
| $166 | 30 days net/2% on | | 60 days net/no |
| | any A/R over 30 days | | additional percentage |
| $10,000 | $100,000 | | $90,000 |
| $500 | 8 week delivery | | 4 week delivery |
| $500 | 1 in-house workshop | | 4 in-house workshops |
| $150 | Annual review report | | Bi-annual review report |
| $13,766 | Cost of Service | Delta | Cost of Service |

*Take 2 minutes and fill in the "Delta" between what Your Proposal and what the Client Wants. Based on the exercise, which elements will have the largest financial impact on your negotiation.*

**STEP ONE:** _____

**STEP TWO:** _____

**STEP THREE:** _____

**STEP FOUR:** _____

**STEP FIVE:** _____

**STEP SIX:** _____

| Cost | Your Proposal | | Client Wants |
|---|---|---|---|
| $_____/yr. | ___% rebate | | ___% rebate |
| $_____/yr. | ___ free service calls | | ___ free service calls |
| $_____/yr. | ___ days net/___% on any A/R over ___ days | | ___ days net/no additional percentage |
| $_____ | $_____ | | $_____ |
| $_____ | ___ week delivery | | ___ week delivery |
| $_____ | ___ in-house workshop | | ___ in-house workshops |
| $_____ | Annual review report | | Bi-annual review report |
| $_____ | _____ | | _____ |
| $_____ | _____ | | _____ |
| $_____ | _____ | | _____ |
| $_____ | **Cost of Service** | **Delta** | **Cost of Service** |

# NEGOTIATING TIPS

## NEGOTIATE AND GAIN AGREEMENT

Once we present our solutions to clients, we may be called upon to negotiate as we each pursue an agreement. Sooner or later, every sale comes down to a series of discussions that finalize the deal. The issues to be resolved may include final pricing or other terms. But in all cases, both the sales person and the customer want to move forward. This is the point where your negotiation skills come to the forefront.

Please review when preparing for the final negotiation. Whether you are involved in complex or simple negotiations, the following list of negotiation concepts may be helpful.

| NEGOTIATION SUGGESTIONS |
|---|
| **1** Listen closely. The other party will give you valuable information to help you reach an agreement. |
| **2** Know where you want to go. Set your goals for the negotiation, and know how much you are able to bend on all key issues. |
| **3** Aim high. The higher you aim, the higher you will end up... but don't insult the client. |
| **4** Consider deadlines. Deadline pressure causes people to make concessions more willingly. Avoid this pitfall yourself, and capitalize on it where possible. |
| **5** Don't be afraid of deadlock—when appropriate. People have an inherent desire for closure. Don't give in to this tendency. Your willingness to walk away from a negotiation is the only true leverage you have. |
| **6** Use a co-operative approach for win-win results. Seek the best, mutually-satisfying solution in every negotiation, if you want to maintain in a long-standing partnership with your clients. Ensure that no party "loses" in the negotiation. |
| **7** Look for a better deal. Even once you believe you have an agreement... there may be a way to make it even better for both parties. Look to the secondary issues from the negotiation to find even better solutions. |
| **8** Ask. Listen. And don't talk too much. Successful negotiators spend most of their time asking questions, versus speaking. |
| **9** Resist concessions, but secure them from customers. Ensure concessions are small, and reluctantly given. |
| **10** Allow your opponent to save face. When your customer says, "That's the best I can do..." offer them some small, inconsequential concession to you, enabling them to save face when making another concession. |
| **11** Use compliance tactics, and avoid them yourself. The Compliance Tactics introduced in the Professional Selling program can be helpful in securing customer movement...but avoid falling prey to them yourself. |

# LESSONS FROM THE ROAD

Purchasing has evolved over the past 25 years. It was extremely rare that Purchasing (or Procurement or Buying Department) could halt a sale once the KDM or Committee has approved a purchase.

However, many organizations now have a separate purchasing department that negotiates after the KDM or Committee has approved. In many cases they squeeze an additional margin out of the transaction and, over the course of the year, become significant contributors to their own firm's bottom line.

Earlier in my career I was at our company's training centre in Leesburg, Virgina. The centre was highly respected and both company employees and clients would attend intensive training in sales and sales management.

While there, I noticed lots of US Marine Corps soldiers also attending the training sessions. Curious, I asked one of them what they were doing at our sales training centre. His answer made me laugh. 'Sir' he said, 'I am a recruiter with the US Marine Corps'. So, why are you here?' I asked. Sir' he said 'I am taking sales training'. 'Why is a US Marine taking sales training I asked'. He smiled and said 'Sir, if I can sell a guy to give me 3 years of his life, I can sell him anything!'

I discovered that not only recruiters but buyers; purchasing department executives and procurement specialists were all attending our training.

Never forget that while you are studying their negotiation techniques... they are studying yours!

PLANNING
TEAM
FUNDS
IDEA
CROWD SOURCED
LEADERSHIP
GROWTH
PLAN B
EXIT

# POP QUIZ – PURCHASING APPROVES

Time to test your knowledge on the preceding material with the Quota POP QUIZ! 10 questions at each POP QUIZ. Try to answer without looking at the chapter and give yourself a maximum of 2 minutes to complete the quiz.

## 1 POINT QUESTION IF CORRECT

1) True or False: Purchasing may be interested in expediting payment for additional discounts?

T) True
F ) False

ANSWER: ........................

2) Steps to successful negotiations include:

a. Defining the current situation
b. Reviewing the benefits of the proposed solution?
c. Confirm the existing 'gap' between what is needed/offered?
d. All of the above

ANSWER: ........................

3) True or False: The strongest negotiating tactic is to make your best offer and then walk away?

T) True
F ) False

ANSWER: ........................

4) Negotiating tactics include:

a. Speaking without waiting to hear client's thoughts
b. Being the only party to offer solutions
c. Reinforce finding a 'win/win' solution
d. All of the above

ANSWER: ........................

5) True or False: At this advanced stage the purchase is guaranteed?

T) True
F ) False

ANSWER: ........................

6) True or False: Once the KDM/Committee has approved a sale, purchasing must approve as well?

      T) True

      F ) False

                                          ANSWER: ......................

7) A strategy to garner purchasing support is to:

      a. Put on more pressure

      b. Have the influencer argue with them

      c. Make a separate presentation to them

      d. All of the above

                                          ANSWER: ......................

8) True or False: Purchasing Departments have their own cost containment objectives?

      T) True

      F ) False

                                          ANSWER: ......................

9) Steps in the client's 'Buying Cycle' may include:

      a. Sourcing Competitive Bids

      b. Seeing a product/service demonstration

      c. Speak with current users of the product/service

      d. All of the above

                                          ANSWER: ......................

10) When purchasing becomes an obstacle to your sale, it is best to:

      a. Solicit KDM/Committee support

      b. Argue with the senior purchasing executive

      c. Offer them gifts

      d. None of the above

                                          ANSWER: ......................

# PURCHASING APPROVES

                      FINAL SCORE: _____ / 10

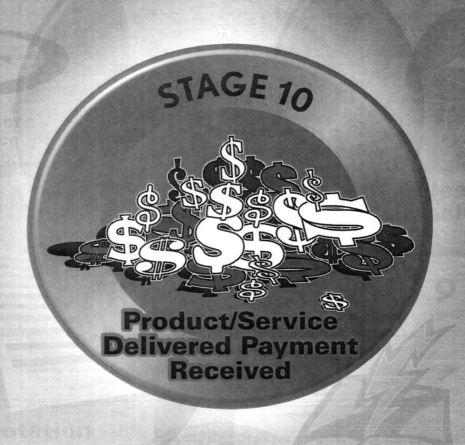

**STAGE 10**

**Product/Service Delivered Payment Received**

POST SALE SERVICE— THIS IS WHERE PARTNERSHIP TRULY COMES INTO PLAY!

# stage ten

## PRODUCT/SERVICE DELIVERED PAYMENT RECEIVED

It is often said: "Beware what you wish for." We all want to make a sale, but also need to be prepared for what takes place after the sale. Clients and situations are fluid and even the most innocuous delivery of products/services can be beset by unforeseen problems and obstacles.

## POST-SALE SERVICE

This is where partnership truly comes into play. Your commitment to ensuring your client receives all the benefits you described in the sales process will be measured at this stage. Some simple post-sale follow-up activities include:

- Contact your clients when delivery of product/service is confirmed.
- Thank them again for the opportunity to do business with them.
- Provide them your direct coordinates should there be any breakdowns in service.
- Schedule a follow up phone call mid-delivery to review their impressions.
- Schedule a follow up meeting post-delivery to review implementation.
- Thank your Manager and have a quiet celebration! Every achievement should be recognized and celebrated. Celebrations will keep you positive during times of rejection, so don't overlook them!

These basic steps will provide your clients with a secure feeling they have chosen well and that there will be a direct contact should anything not transpire as promised. From your viewpoint, not only will you set a high bar for any competitor to jump over, you will also further integrate your product/service into your client's organization and be in an ideal position to spot future business potential!

# PRODUCT/SERVICE DELIVERED

## THANK YOUR CLIENT

Although this seems like a simple step...it is astonishing how often it does not happen. At this stage of the selling process, your client has come to know you and know your company. Somewhere in the process, they decided they trusted you and what your product/service could do for their company. They also decided you could do it better than someone else.

A simple gesture (hand-written note, email, or phone call) to say "thank you" for the trust invested in you is always noted and appreciated. The cost to say "thank you" is small. The consequence of not saying "thank you" could be enormous!

## PERSONALIZE YOUR THANK YOU.

# LESSONS FROM THE ROAD

As a leading sales training company we conducted some insightful market surveys in the late 1990's. With the advent of Just-in-time (JIT) purchasing, our concern was that client's may not feel a need to have professional salespeople anymore.

Technology seemed to reducing the 'hands on' service aspect of managing our clients and even online bidding was gaining popularity. The key question was "Will you have a need for professional salespeople to manage your account in the coming years?".

The good news was that our clients resoundingly responded that - 'Yes, we want and need professional salespeople' Their rationale was that technology was actually making more difficult to know where/when and how to best implement their purchase.

### However, they also provided 3 caveats:

1) We only want one point of contact. We termed this person the 'Strategic Orchestrator'. They understood that this point of contact would not be the expert in all areas of the implementation. But they only wanted to call one person...who in turn would bring in the experts as needed.

2) We expect the point of contact to know our business. We will provide minimal time to educating them but we expect that they already have industry insight or experience.

3) We want transparency in all our transactions. We don't want to be involved in extensive negotiating each time we do business. We want to know your costs/margins and we will jointly create a long-term, mutually profitable relationship that allows both parties to succeed.

# POP QUIZ - REVIEW

Time to test your knowledge on the preceding material with the Quota POP QUIZ! 10 questions at each POP QUIZ. Try to answer without looking at the chapter and give yourself a maximum of 2 minutes to complete the quiz.

## 1 POINT QUESTION IF CORRECT

1) True or False: Once we have secured the sale there is no need for us to remain in contact with our client?
   - T) True
   - F ) False

   ANSWER: ............................

2) Client communication at this stage should include:
   - a. A written timeline of events/deliverables
   - b. Your vacation plans
   - c. Commitment to advance without needing a P.O.
   - d. None of the above

   ANSWER: ............................

3) True or False: There is no need to communicate internally until the order is immediately due?
   - T) True
   - F ) False

   ANSWER: ............................

4) Thanking a client can be done:
   - a. Verbally
   - b. Email
   - c. Hand-written note
   - d. All of the above

   ANSWER: ............................

5) Elements of a professional quotation should include:
   - a  Detailed information on competitive quotations
   - b. Multiple pricing variations
   - c. Open ended quotation
   - d. None of the above

   ANSWER: ............................

6) When working with an Executive Assistant, we should:
   a. See if they have access to their boss' agenda
   b. Get and use their first name
   c. Don't push on the first call
   d. All of the above

   **ANSWER:** _____

7) Three elements in leaving a successful message include:
   a. Same day call back
   b. One time to contact us
   c. Phone number first
   d. None of the above

   **ANSWER:** _____

8) Is selling an art or a science?
   a. Art
   b. Science
   c. Both
   d. Neither

   **ANSWER:** _____

9) 5 Potential sources of leads may include:
   a. Trade associations
   b. Personal contacts
   c. Cold calls
   d. All of the above

   **ANSWER:** _____

10) How do you respond to a client that says 'Send me a brochure':
    a. No - I have more questions
    b. OK - what is your email address?
    c. I would love to but our products/services are quite complex. May I
       ask you a few more questions to know which brochure to send?
    d. None of the above

    **ANSWER:** _____

11) What are the three Organization Motivators?
   a. Cultural, Objectives, Financial
   b. Contextual, Observational, Forward-looking
   c. Cultural, Operational, Futuristic
   d. None of the above

   **ANSWER:** ........................

12) What are the three levels in a prospect funnel:
   a. Acquisition, Expansion, Retention
   b. Acquisition, Expansion, Returning
   c. Awareness, Expulsion, Retention
   d. None of the above

   **ANSWER:** ........................

13) True or False: Is improved safety for your family a benefit?
   T) True
   F ) False

   **ANSWER:** ........................

14) True or False: Is a warranty a benefit?
   T) True
   F ) False

   **ANSWER:** ........................

15) List 4 of the closing styles:
   a. Direct, Indirect, Begging, Crying
   b. Suggestive, Intuitive, Supported, Stepped
   c. Direct, Narrative, Supported, Alternative
   d. None of the above

   **ANSWER:** ........................

# REVIEW
**FINAL SCORE:** _____ / 15

# POP QUIZ ANSWERS!

POP QUIZ # 1 - KEY EVENTS:          A, D, C, D, F

                                                                    ___/5

POP QUIZ # 2 - PROSPECTING:          C, F, C, D, T, D F, B C, F

                                                                    ___/10

POP QUIZ # 3 - INITIAL MEETING:          A, F, A, A, F, D, D, D, D, F

                                                                    ___/10

POP QUIZ # 4- NEEDS ANALYSIS:          D, F, B, T, T, C, F, C, D, T

                                                                    ___/10

POP QUIZ # 5 - PRODUCT/          D, A, T, D, F, T, D, C, F, F
SERVICE DEMO:
                                                                    ___/10

POP QUIZ # 6 - QUOTATION:          T, B, T, A, F, F, D, T, C, D

                                                                    ____/10

POP QUIZ # 7 - INFLUENCER          C, T, A, C, F, T, D, C, B, T
APPROVES:
                                                                    ____/10

POP QUIZ # 8 - KDM/COMMITTEE          F, C, F, C, T, F, D, F, D, B
APPROVES:
                                                                    ___/10

POP QUIZ # 9 - PURCHASING          T, D, F, C, F, F, C, T, D, A
APPROVES:
                                                                    ___/10

POP QUIZ # 10 - DELIVERY &          F, A, F, D, D, D, D, C, D, C, C, A, T, F, C
REVIEW:
                                                                    ___/15


                                                TOTAL _____/100

# RESULTS

**Score: 90-100:**
Way to go! You understand the key competencies required to successfully guide your client through the sales process. Next step is to thoroughly understand your client's business environment and link your products/services to their operational objectives.

**Score: 70-89:**
Well done! You have a solid grasp of the key competencies required to successfully guide your client through the sales process. Next step is to ensure you are implementing the key competencies in each stage of the sales process. Review which questions had an incorrect answer and implement the correct response in your upcoming sales calls.

**Score: 50-69:**
Getting there! You understand some of the key competencies required to successfully guide your client through the sales process. More practice is needed to identify the specific areas you answered incorrectly and to incorporate the correct responses in your everyday sales. Remember that sales success is a combination of both skill and art. Improve either and your sales will go up!

**Score: Below 50:**
The first step in any skill acquisition is to first diagnose where you are. Your effort to fill in the questionnaire is an indication you want to get better at these powerful sales competencies. Review all correct/incorrect questions and learn which responses will best help you grow as a professional sales person. Take the quiz again in 3 months time and see the results!

# CONGRATULATIONS!

You are now an Essential Sales - The 10 Steps to Sales Success Graduate and are on your way to increased sales performance and commission dollars! Bring your Skill Review Guide Cards (end of this book) with you on your sales calls and keep the book prominently in your work area. The best way to improve your usage of the skills in the book is to use it as an ongoing personal coach!

As the old saying goes..."The harder I work...the luckier I get." Use the skills contained in this book, keep filling your pipeline, work hard throughout the sales cycle and you will truly have all the luck you require for extraordinary success.

# ESSENTIAL
# SALES

## To contact
## the Authors:

**Earl Robertson:**
iaito1@me.com
(905) 601-2880

**Steven Tulman:**
steven.tulman@gmail.com
(416) 949-7838

# ABOUT THE AUTHORS

EARL
**ROBERTSON**

Earl Robertson is President and Founder of QUOTA® INTERNATIONAL. Earl has had an extensive career in sales, marketing, operations and executive management. Mr. Robertson has been CEO of a multi-million dollar staffing services company, President of an international technical training company and was a former executive with Xerox Learning Systems and top salesperson with Procter & Gamble Inc.

QUOTA® INTERNATIONAL is a leading sales training company with operations in 24 countries and 7 languages. The company has a portfolio of products that provide development and skills in: sales; sales management; sales software; advanced strategic sales; and leadership. QUOTA® INTERNATIONAL is also present in a number of academic institutions internationally and produces the popular Q NEWS™ newsletter that goes out to thousands of readers.

Mr. Robertson has been the driving force for the international expansion of QUOTA® INTERNATIONAL. He spends each year visiting his international operations and has in-depth experience with international business and key account management.

He is a graduate in business from Concordia University in Montreal and has achieved the CERTIFIED SALES PROFESSIONAL (with distinction) from the Canadian Professional Sales Association. He has also served as a Business Advisor to the Concordia University Faculty of Commerce and is a Lead Judge at the annual INTERNATIONAL MBA CASE STUDY COMPETITION. Mr. Robertson is also an Instructor for Professional Sales and Sales Management at the University of Toronto, School of Continuing Studies and a guest lecturer on Sales in various academic institutions. Mr. Robertson has also served on a variety of Boards (public and private).

STEVEN
**TULMAN**

Steven Tulman is the Co-Founder and CEO of Social Pulse Marketing Inc., a top Influencer and Social Media Marketing agency.

Over the years, Steven has developed, led, and executed successful marketing and sales strategies that have helped organizations in the retail, consumer services, technology, finance, hospitality and not for profit sectors scale their operations and increase revenues.

In addition to helping companies with their sales and growth strategies, Steven also conducts regular sales, marketing, and management workshops for major global organizations, top universities and colleges, and conferences.

His profound experience developing and executing highly successful sales teams for a variety of different industries and verticals empowers him with the knowledge and ability to ensure that companies receive significant ROI on their sales training investment.

In his spare time, Steven enjoys sports, the arts, travelling the world, and actively working with education-based and youth empowering charities.

*the end*